1600 TRUMP AVENUE

AGAINST ALL ODDS

A Political Prophecy

For my favorite yankee !

Greg

LES PENDLETON

Essie Press

Palm Coast Services, Inc. dba **Essie Press**
901 Sawgrass Court
New Bern, NC 28560
www.essiepress.com
EMAIL: essie-press@lespendleton.com

This book is a work of fiction. The characters, names, incidents, dialogue and plot are the products of the author's imagination or are used fictitiously. Any resemblance to actual persons or events is purely coincidental. Some of the people and places in the book are real, though actions and events are all works of fiction.

ISBN Paperback: 978-0-9754740-4-4
Ebook: 978-0-9754740-5-1

Cover by Damonza

Author photo by Robert Dumon Photography

To my wife, Susanne Harrison Pendleton. Her unshakable love and support, coupled with her limitless enthusiasm for life, keeps me going.

Acknowledgments

Thank you to Jim Grimshaw, a very real retired Army Ranger. He epitomizes what a patriot should be.

Thank you to Donald Trump, the first "people's choice" for President in my lifetime.

Excerpts from President Dwight D. Eisenhower's farewell address to the nation

This speech was delivered in a television broadcast on January 17, 1961. It was his final public speech as President of the United States.

"We now stand ten years past the midpoint of a century that has witnessed four major wars among great nations. Three of these involved our own country. Despite these holocausts, America is today the strongest, the most influential and most productive nation in the world. Understandably proud of this pre-eminence, we yet realize that America's leadership and prestige depend, not merely upon our unmatched material progress, riches and military strength, but on how we use our power in the interests of world peace and human betterment.

"Until the latest of our world conflicts, the United States had no armaments industry. American makers of plowshares could, with time and as required, make swords as well. But now we can no longer risk emergency improvisation of national defense; we have been compelled to create a permanent armaments industry of vast proportions. Added to this, three and a half million men and women are directly engaged in the defense establishment. We annually spend on military security more than the net income of all United States corporations.

"This conjunction of an immense military establishment and a large arms industry is new in the American experience. The total influence -- economic, political, even spiritual -- is felt in every city, every State house, every office of the Federal government.

We recognize the imperative need for this development. Yet we must not fail to comprehend its grave implications. Our toil, resources and livelihood are all involved; so is the very structure of our society.

"In the councils of government, we must guard against the acquisition of unwarranted influence, whether sought or unsought, by the military industrial complex. The potential for the disastrous rise of misplaced power exists and will persist.

"We must never let the weight of this combination endanger our liberties or democratic processes. We should take nothing for granted. Only an alert and knowledgeable citizenry can compel the proper meshing of the huge industrial and military machinery of defense with our peaceful methods and goals, so that security and liberty may prosper together.

"Disarmament, with mutual honor and confidence, is a continuing imperative. Together we must learn how to compose differences, not with arms, but with intellect and decent purpose. Because this need is so sharp and apparent I confess that I lay down my official responsibilities in this field with a definite sense of disappointment. As one who has witnessed the horror and the lingering sadness of war -- as one who knows that another war could utterly destroy this civilization which has been so slowly and painfully built over thousands of years -- I wish I could say tonight that a lasting peace is in sight."

Prologue

Anger had taken over the country. America was divided. Nothing seemed to be in order and the country was in a tailspin. Eight years after an unvetted, socialist candidate was elected to the Presidency promising positive change, anything but that had occurred. The economy was in shambles for the average person. Government leaders and Wall Street were doing incredibly well, while the rest of the nation suffered. Crime was rampant. Being seen as racists or bigots, the police had almost given up. The country's borders had been eradicated to the point they were nothing more than an open door offering access to anyone wanting to come in, regardless of their country of origin or even their criminal past. The Attorney General had become a puppet of the Executive Branch and prosecuted only those who were of a different political persuasion than the President. The media appeared to be doing all it could to promote anything the average American abhorred. Even churches seemed to be caving in to political correctness, refusing to take a stand on anything, no matter how immoral or contrary to church teachings it might be. The great universities had become a cesspool where many liberal-minded instructors taught that anything anti-American was correct, while not tolerating even the smallest voice to the contrary among the students entrusted to them.

Middle America had endured enough. Unfortunately, there seemed to be no avenue left for them to push back. At work, at school, in public offices or even at social gatherings, extremists had successfully made it very risky to voice any sort of opposition to their view of how the country should be run. The mainstream media had also become the extremist's personal advertising agency. The media became devoted to reporting on the outlandish viewpoints and lifestyles of a small percentage of people living in America, while devaluing traditional American family values. They had been disenfranchised by an extreme fringe minority who dared them to take any sort of stand against them. No one even tried to speak up. That applied especially to the political class. That was until a brash, outspoken billionaire businessman named Donald Trump announced he was a candidate for President of the United States. Considered by many to be only a television personality because of his starring role in a reality show, he was downplayed by the complicit media as a clown and a huckster. However, he didn't need the elite power brokers to run for office. He had plenty of his own money and couldn't be silenced by a system that millions of Americans considered broken and corrupt. Donald offered them a last shot at taking back their country and reigning in the radical leaders who seemed to have taken control of every institution in their country. No one ever doubted for a moment how much Donald loved his country and its people. He was unabashed in his devotion to America, its traditions and the potential that lived in the heart of every American to succeed. He knew America could be great once more and he inspired the people to want to win again. There were things he said that made even his most fervent supporters uncomfortable at times, but he always spoke from his heart, with no teleprompter or prepared speeches. He had no political consultants spoon-feeding him sound bites or advisors telling him what was acceptable in the political environment of the time. Donald was a breath of fresh air for many who felt there was no oxygen left for them. They would back him to the end if he would look out for the values they wanted to see reinstated in their country, their government, their institutions and their leaders. America needed to go back to its roots before those roots could no longer be found. Donald Trump offered them that opportunity and they wouldn't let it pass.

1

November 8, 2016 – Election Day

Professor R. Jeffrey Burroughs was one of the oldest professors on campus at the Wharton School of the University of Pennsylvania. Tall and thin with a thick crop of unruly white hair, he stood with a slight stoop and walked with a cane. Arthritis was taking a toll on his hips and standing a full hour for lectures several times each day was becoming more difficult. He knew he was nearing the end of his career. His life had been teaching at Wharton for almost forty years. Many of the students now in attendance considered him to be a dinosaur, a far right ideologue with whom they had nothing in common. They thought his ideas were stale, assuming the only possible reason he was still allowed to teach was tenure and some well-received books he had written decades before their arrival. Nonetheless, to graduate they must listen to him drone on with his business theories intermingled with his thoughts about just where the world was headed and how that path came to be. Today, he was on a tangent talking about the presidential election that was under way at the voting booths. The leading candidate in almost every poll conducted over the past year was a former student of his named Donald Trump. Many of his former students had gone on to become titans in the business world, but Trump was the first to ever run for President of the United States of America.

"And today, he will most likely be elected President. Do any of you illustrious political voyeurs have any idea how an outsider, a man whose candidacy was considered to be a joke by the political elite less than a year ago, wound up as your next President? How is this possible? I'd love your opinions. Speak up. Don't be shy. Whatever you say here is fine. After all, we're still guaranteed freedom of speech, aren't we? Stacy, I see you are the bravest in my class. What say ye about Donald Trump?"

The young woman expounded with the confident air of the far left-leaning cultural elite that she and her parent's' money had fostered in her.

"He's a jerk. A smart ass. I don't think he's very intelligent either."

"I see, Stacy, then how do you explain his appeal to so many?"

"Most Americans are stupid. I'm sorry. They can't do well in society because they don't understand how anything actually works. They're mad about their own failure and along comes a snake oil salesman who promises to fix everything about society that holds them down. Bam, they're sold. He plays to their anger at society even though every problem they have is of their own making. We need an intellectual in the White House. Trump will fail miserably because he doesn't really have any idea about what he's doing."

"Thank you, Stacy. I see you have thought about this quite a bit. I'm certain that many others in this classroom share those feelings with you. In fact, I'd bet most of you share her viewpoint. Well, my thoughts are very different than yours. Since I'm the instructor and you need a good grade from my class, I trust you will humor me and listen, with disdain of course, to my point of view. First, I'd like to say that people are not necessarily poor because they are stupid or lazy. Life is far too complicated to explain poverty away by merely saying 'you're poor, so thus you must be dumb.' Many of these poor people do things like fix your car, mow your lawn, pick up your trash, wear police and firemen uniforms and last but not least, fight your wars. Without them, whether you appreciate it or not, you wouldn't be here today. There would be no cars or buses to ride on your way here. You'd have no food to eat once you got here, and you'd be lucky to make it home without getting robbed. A great many of those people will be voting for Donald Trump today. Some of you may know that he was a student here at Wharton. He took several classes under me. He was a brilliant student. He was interested in learning everything he could about the free market system, capitalism, and how they interplayed on the world market. He embraced a society where a poor person with the desire to rise up through the ranks economically could do so through their own efforts. Granted, he came from a wealthy family himself. His father owned a number of low-income housing projects in New York. He could afford the best schools. Wharton is certainly one of those schools. How many of you in this classroom are paying your own way through school with no help from your parents or other family members? Let's see a show of hands. I don't see any going up. Don't feel bad. That's the case with almost every student that comes here for an education. Therefore, your family, or whoever is paying for your education, is shelling out over a thousand dollars a week for you to be here. Without their financial backing, I'm afraid I wouldn't know a lot of your names. We would have never met. Thus, whether you agree with that premise or not, you are the privileged elite. For every one of you in this classroom today, there are millions of people throughout the world who cannot attend here because there is no one willing or able to pay for it for them. You need to bear all of this in mind when you start calling other people stupid and uninformed. A lot of people you think fit into that category, raise and feed their families without help from anyone. They do their best to see they are warm, dry and safe. They have hopes for their children just like your parents have for you, and just like you may one day have for your own. To group them into predetermined classes based on your own stereotypes is, to me, a sin. Trump's appeal is not coming from stupid people. It's coming from ordinary people who have to work hard to make a living and they see it getting more difficult every day. Their take-home income is disappearing at an alarming rate while taxes and everything else is going up. They don't feel like they have control over any of these factors. Government has become absolutely unresponsive to them except when it needs to collect their tax dollars. It really doesn't want to pay attention to or have any dealings with the unwashed masses. You're right about one thing. They're mad. In fact, they're very mad. For years, only the political elite picked who would run for office. Without their backing, no candidate could finance a run at the Presidency. Now, along comes Donald Trump. Here's a guy who's willing and able to finance his own campaign completely. He doesn't need the endorsement or the money from the established political class. He's smart, extremely successful, a graduate of this fine institution and yet he can speak their language. You might say he's an opportunist. That's fair. He realized this huge group of people was left out of the system as it consistently played favorites every step of the way. As a stagnant economy has placed more and more people among their ranks, their numbers are legion now. The rigged system has created its own demise. Many hard-working but disenfranchised people will have their voices heard today. And by the way, when Mr. Trump attended here, there were several students who were struggling to pay these high tuition costs. Without being asked, he arranged for tuition funding for at least four students, that I know of, to continue their education here. Those students graduated and are doing very well in their careers. To this day, they don't realize that a future President of the United States paid for their tuition. I hope some of you will have the intellect to think a little about what I've told you here today. There's more to be done when you leave here than stockpiling your 401K. Class dismissed."

2

The Beltway Tavern was jammed to capacity despite the awful November weather. The usual ensemble of pool shooters and dart throwers were focused in on their chosen sports, while another group of patrons tried to listen over the gamer's banter to one of the large flat-screen televisions mounted behind the bar. The news anchor was giving an update on exit polls and election results in one of the most controversial presidential elections in modern times.

"And now, let's go to Brian Kercey in one of the outlying precincts here in our nation's capital. Brian, what are you hearing with your impromptu exit polling?"

The reporter was bundled up against a hard wind intermixed with some occasional sleet. "Yes, Sam, I'm personally very surprised, just like all of you, at the huge turnout we've seen in spite of some of the worst Election Day weather any of us can remember. It's also interesting to see the wide diversity of these voters. They're young, old, white, black, Hispanic, white-collar, blue-collar, you name it. It's pretty much a broad cross-section of the country. I've been asking them some questions as they exited the polls. Here's a video showing a few of those answers."

A black man in his early thirties wearing a Washington Redskins cap and a heavy coat paused to give the reporter a quick response. "No, I don't have any problem answering that question. I voted for Donald Trump."

"Any particular thing about Mr. Trump that drew you to him?"

"Absolutely. I've lived here in D.C. for about ten years. I've heard hundreds of politicians make a billion promises. Not just Republican or Democrat, all of them. They say this; they say that; they make all kind of promises and nothing ever changes. Nothing. They all hated Mr. Trump because he ain't one of them and he don't need them. He's got his own money. He don't have to go hat in hand to their party leaders and beg for the money to run. They're all scared of him. He says a lot of things that even I don't like hearing, but I like him because he ain't one of them."

Kercey came back on camera, wiping frozen raindrops from his forehead. "By the way, that gentleman was a D.C. cabbie. As we all know, they never seem to be at a loss for words or an opinion. But I have to tell you, he pretty much echoes what we've been hearing here all afternoon. Here's another."

This time it was an older woman peeking out from her hooded raincoat. Strands of wet silver hair stuck to the side of her face. She had obviously been asked the same question. "Trump. Trump all the way. He'll be the next President and then maybe we can clean out this cesspool we call our government. I know what some people say about him, and I don't care. There's no way he could do any worse than what we've had and to tell you the truth, I trust him. He doesn't use a teleprompter with a bunch of pre-written, politically correct baloney. He speaks what's on his mind as he thinks of it and he doesn't care what anybody thinks. Like him or hate him, he's going to be in charge soon. I can't wait."

"There you have it, Sam. I could play four or five more interviews for you but they're pretty much the same. I think you get the picture."

"So, from what you're seeing, you think Trump will win?"

"If the rest of the country is duplicating what we're seeing here, I think that will be the case. Back to you, Sam."

"There you have it, folks, right from the mouths of the voters. Now let's cut to our panel of experts to see what they make of all this."

A loud cheer broke out from the patrons gathered at the bar. A lone beer drinker near the front door of the bar tried to yell over them, "You idiots don't know what you've done. Washington will have him for breakfast. He's a crook, a billionaire con artist."

"Somebody buy the kid another beer and shut him up. The real people who built this country are having their say today and his side can go pound sand."

* * *

The cold rain continued as the evening wore on. The lobby of the Mayflower Hotel was full to capacity with reporters, TV camera crews, fans and gawkers trying to catch a glimpse of Donald Trump and his wife, Melania, as they entered. Word had spread over the past hour that they would be arriving soon to address a large gathering of supporters, presumably with a victory speech.

"Limos are pulling up," someone shouted above the crowd. "They're here!"

Several black SUVs sporting government plates and carrying members of the Secret Service exited the vehicles in front and behind the stretch limo carrying Trump, his wife, and his lifelong friend and soon-to-be Chief of Staff, Andre Whittal. The two had joined forces during Trump's days at Wharton. Their non-elitist status may have left them out of certain circles at school and even later in the business world. However, the alliance they had forged carried them much farther than those who thought somehow they didn't merit inclusion in their special group. Behind the dark tinted windows, Donald Trump addressed his friend.

"You first, Andre. Stick a foot in the water and tell me how cold it is."

"You mean get blinded by all the camera crews."

"Whatever. Let's do this."

They exited the limo and walked briskly to the front door of the grand hotel. Despite the rain, there were reporters shooting off questions as they walked past them.

"Are you a lock now, Donald?"

"Have you heard from your opponent? Has she called to concede yet?"

Donald just raised his hand with a gesture of greeting as they passed. There was barely a pathway through the lobby as they followed Secret Service agents toward an elevator that was being held open by hotel staff and already occupied by two agents. Donald paused for a moment in the center of the room.

"Thank you all for being here. It's a rough night out there and I appreciate your turning out to support us. I assume that's why most of you are here. A lot of folks, a tremendous amount of folks, came out to vote today. I think we'll have an announcement for you very shortly. Thank you all again."

Donald, Melania and Andre, trailed by other staffers and guards made their way through the crowd to the elevator and proceeded to the hotel's largest suite on the top floor of the prestigious venue. Events like this were nothing new to the

Mayflower. Built in 1925, the Mayflower had been host to almost every politician, socialite and celebrity that ever visited the nation's capital, from Roosevelt to Charles Lindbergh and beyond. Donald Trump felt it was the right place to host this evening's events. As they approached the entrance to his suite, two Secret Service agents stood by to greet him and open the door.

"The room is secure, sir. We'll be just outside in the hall. Someone will be right here at all times, while others are securing the convention center and hotel entrances throughout the night."

"I'm very appreciative. You fellows do a fine job."

"Thank you, sir."

"No, I mean it. I'm very proud to have you working on my behalf."

"No problem."

The three of them entered the room.

"They do a great job, don't they?"

"They seem to know what they're doing. I'll say that."

"Absolutely. Anybody here?"

The suite consisted of multiple living areas, the salon, and a kitchen and beyond that a smaller, more intimate sitting area with a wet bar, small dining table and a picture window overlooking downtown Washington, D.C.

A voice came from the adjoining room. "In here, sir. We're just taking your suit out of the dry cleaning bag and turning down your bed. By the way, Ivanka just called. She's with her brother, Donald Jr., and they're on the way here. She says to not go down to the meeting hall without them. They want to see it all with you. They're thrilled about how things are going according to all the news outlets."

"You knew this was going to be the case, didn't you, Brit?"

"Well, I had certainly hoped so. But, I've watched so many elections over the years, listened to polls that were a hundred percent wrong and seen so many people get elected that I thought had no chance so I am never completely sure. But, as usual, Mr. Trump, you are probably going to bring home the trophy tonight."

"It sure looks that way, Brit. It sure does. Andre, let's just take a few minutes and sit down. I want to catch my breath and get my thoughts collected before we go any further."

"Do you want to put some words on paper to use as notes for your speech this evening?"

"You're pretty confident we've got this thing wrapped up, huh?"

"Not a chance you'll lose. You'll need to have some gracious remarks to thank everyone and tell your opponent what a great lady she really is."

"Right. A really great woman. It's a shame she's the highest-ranking subordinate to Lucifer. I'll just say we spoke. That is, if she even calls to acknowledge we ate her for lunch. As far as any prepared remarks, you know that's not how I like to do business. People aren't that stupid. They understand that folks who read everything as they say it aren't speaking from the heart. They're just the mouthpiece for an agenda being directed by those who own them. My supporters made it pretty clear how they felt about that. I'll just thank everyone for coming and ask for their continuing support. With the changes I'm going after, I will need the public to be with me. A tremendous amount of folks working up here are going to hate me even more than they already do."

"You know, to them you're not just the hope for the country, you're the face of a threat to their livelihood, which they thought would be around forever."

"Ah, yes. The bureaucracy. The millions and millions of highly-paid government workers that spend most of every day trying to find and explain the reason they're being paid to do whatever the hell it is they do. They have a reason to be concerned. I'm going after every department up here. They're going to have to explain to me in very simple terms just what they do for us and why we need to keep paying them. I understand fully why the public has supported me. For years, they've been pushed around by a government that considers its biggest mandate to be its own continued growth and taking control of every part of their life, especially their money. And they've managed to set up the system so anyone who's not on their side can't even run. Every state's election rules are designed to keep the two parties in power."

"You sure got around that, sir."

"All we've done so far is just get hired. Now we need to see if we can turn this whole can of worms around. I know we'll be up against resistance beyond our wildest expectations. I'm prepared to deal with that."

"They've chosen the right man for the job."

"We'll see, Andre. We'll see."

Brit, the bright-eyed, young woman Donald had hired straight out of Princeton to help with event scheduling, came over to where the men were seated. Melania went into the bedroom to start getting ready for the night's big event.

"Mr. Trump, before you start to get ready, do you have a moment to meet Mrs. Eason, Jeremy's mother? You remember she's invited to the event this evening and will be on stage to your left side?"

"Of course I want to see her. I thought a lot of Jeremy. Still can't believe such a fine young man died so senselessly."

Jeremy Eason was a young campaign staff member who had been killed while driving the campaign's tour bus to an event.

"Thank God he was on his way to pick us up and the bus was empty or a lot more of our staff and friends could have been seriously injured. Bring her in. I'd like to have a few words with her."

The middle-aged woman entered the room. She was still hurting tremendously from the loss of her only son. Donald and Andre stood to greet her. Donald immediately walked across the room and gave her a warm embrace.

"Mrs. Eason. Thank you for being here this evening. I can only imagine how difficult this has to be for you. Will your husband be here as well?"

"No, sir. I'm a widow. Mr. Eason died of cancer a number of years ago. It was just me and Jeremy. He so hoped you would become President. He believed in you with all his heart."

"I spoke with him a number of times and he was an articulate, bright, and warm young man. Jeremy had a big future ahead of him. To lose him so young is not only an awful loss for you as his mother, but it's a tremendous loss for everyone who knew him as well. I want to mention him tonight in my speech if you don't mind."

"It would be an honor, Mr. Trump. I'm sorry... I can't quit crying. "

"That's completely understandable. Brit, get some tissue for Mrs. Eason and some water. Could you use a glass of water?"

"No, just some tissue."

Brit handed her a small box of tissues.

"Here, keep this. You might want some with you on stage, later. I'll have Brit show you the waiting room downstairs where you will be comfortable. If you need anything at all, just call me. Either I'll come down or send someone."

Donald hugged her once more. "Mrs. Eason, thank you again for being here. I'll see you shortly."

Donald walked with her to the door. As she left, he remarked to Andre. "What a senseless tragedy. Such a shame."

Donald and Andre small talked about their early times together and the paths they had taken that brought them to this momentous evening. Despite the grueling year of nonstop campaign speeches and interviews, traveling, hotel rooms and restaurant food, both men were still full of adrenalin for what they knew would be a life-changing event unfolding tonight. They both shared one serious concern. Donald's Vice President would be William Snowden. It wasn't Donald's idea. Andre could see Donald's brow rise in disgust at the mention of his name.

"So, is Snowden going to be here tonight as well?"

"I don't think he'd miss anything where there's a spotlight for him to get under. He's been the biggest thorn in my side throughout this entire process. He's not who I would have chosen. The party pretty much insisted. They thought there was no way I'd carry the western states without him. First off, he's a retired general. What kind of experience is that to run the world's largest economy? All a general knows is the government prints money and hands it over to the Pentagon. Whatever he gets, he spends. The country is going broke with millions on food stamps and welfare. The biggest war we're going to have is how to trim back all the entitlements the government is shelling out every month. A general is going to know how to rein that in? Really? Plus, I don't trust the guy. He's a snake. If the party leaders loved him, then I don't have any reason to trust him. They'd have done anything to keep a non-politician like me out of the White House. We're disrupting their carefully-laid plans. I want you to help me keep a close watch on Snowden. You see or smell anything that doesn't seem right, let me know pronto."

"I'm with you on Snowden. Didn't like him or trust him from day one. I'll be watching everything he does."

Brit walked back in the room, phone in hand. "It's Hillary Clinton, the call you've been waiting for."

Donald walked over to a stuffed leather chair, took his time as he sat down. He took a sip of water from a glass on the adjacent end table, slowly crossed his legs and looked at the receiver as he placed it to his ear. It was obvious that he was savoring the moment. "Mrs. Clinton. How are you this evening?"

"Well, Donald, it's not been the best day for me as I'm sure you are aware. You did it. You got enough disillusioned and bitter people to vote for you. I just hope you're not naive enough to think you'll be able to do one percent of the things you've promised them. But, when you're running for office, I guess anything you say that helps you win is fair game."

"I'm surprised and a little hurt by your accusations, Hillary. May I call you Hillary?"

"If you must."

"OK, no problem, Mrs. Clinton it is. I assume you're calling to offer me your best wishes and recognize that we've won?"

"I do concede that it's over and you won. However, my best wishes will not be forthcoming. The lies you and your henchmen have spread about me will be causing me problems including untold legal bills for years to come. Have a nice evening."

"I will, Mrs. Clinton, and thanks for the call."

Andre smiled as he addressed the obvious. "Not a pleasant concession I take it?"

"About what I would have expected. She's a woman with a lot of problems staring her in the face. If you spend a lifetime handling snakes, no matter how careful you are, you're eventually going to get bitten. Unfortunately, in politics, those bites are usually expensive and fatal. I don't wish her any harm. I'm just glad to be seeing her in the rear view mirror."

More key staff members started to enter the room with regularity. Most were smiling and patting each other on the back. Jeff Styron, Donald's communications director, came over and hugged him as if they hadn't seen each other in years.

"You did it. You took on the entire bunch of Washington establishment politicians, crooks, pundits and hacks and kicked their butts!"

"*We* did it, Jeff. Everyone in this room and a lot of good people all across the country. They haven't had anyone looking out for them up here for a long time. I told them we'd fix that and they believed me. And guess what? That's exactly what we're going to do. Now, what's the timetable for tonight?"

Andre came over beside him and handed him a piece of paper.

"Here's what I'm thinking. Brit likes it. I was going to let some other staff members go over it all before you to get a consensus, but I'm sure they won't mind if the boss sees it first."

"No problem. You can handle as much as you want to tonight. I want to take in every minute of it, almost like a spectator. Any help is appreciated."

Donald quickly studied the evening's schedule. "Looks fine to me."

He handed it to Andre. "Here. You bless it and it's a go as far as I'm concerned."

As Andre and Jeff took a final look at the document, Donald sat back in the chair, took a deep breath and sipped his glass of water. The door to the room opened as Donald's wife, Melania, walked in, followed by his daughter Ivanka and his son Donald, Jr. Melania was considerably younger than Donald and stunningly attractive. Ivanka was beautiful and carried herself confidently over to her father. She kissed him gently on the cheek. Melania likewise walked over to him, standing just behind him while he remained seated in his chair. She gently placed her hands on either side of his head and he warmly placed his hands on top of hers.

"Congratulations, Donald. If this is really what you wanted, then there's no one happier for you than me.

Donald stood up while still holding one of her hands and explained. "Melania, you know there are a lot of things I'd rather do than this. My first choice would be for you and I to just be alone in our beautiful home in Florida, enjoying the incredible scenery and the weather with no problems, no media, no employees to deal with, just you and me. I'd even prefer to be building a new resort or office tower than to be doing this. But, you know I feel called to save this country. I've seen it under attack all my life from every sort of faction. From greedy politicians and fanatical zealots to religious warriors and dictators. You name it. The country is in serious trouble. Nobody else in Washington even thinks it can be turned around and, honestly, they don't seem to want to. They're making a damn good living on the backs of everyone else. The last thing they want to see is any of their personal apple carts being turned upside down. And darling, that's exactly what I intend to do. I've told everyone that's what I'd do if they elected me and you know how I am when I say I'm going to do something. I'm always a man of my word."

"Unfortunately, yes. I do. So I guess we'll be moving here for a few years?"

"Don't worry, the White House is a nice place, I'll keep a plane close by so that when you've had enough, we can get away."

"Our plane? What about Air Force One?"

"You know, it's not as nice as ours but you're right. That's probably the one we should take."

Brit walked over to the couple. "Mr. President..."

"Not yet, Brit. I have to be sworn in. But, I have to admit, that sounds pretty terrific."

"OK, Mr. Trump. It's time. Take those freshly pressed clothes you're going to wear and put them on because we need to be down in the ballroom within the hour. I'm told it's completely full, standing room only. The Fire Marshall stopped anyone else from entering the room."

"Fabulous, Brit. Come on, Melania. You can make sure I look Presidential."

Knowing that Donald didn't really need that sort of adoration and was merely saying it for effect, she took his arm and walked toward the large bedroom in the back of the suite.

"And I've brought just the right gown to wear as your 'First Lady' for this occasion."

They laughed quietly to each other as they closed the door behind them.

3

The aroma of expensive colognes and perfume filled the air inside the huge ballroom of The Mayflower Hotel. There were so many people in the grand room that the combined mix of banter from individuals and small groups made the room sound like a hometown crowd cheering for the Redskins at a sold out RFK stadium. An up-tempo beat from the rock band on stage added to the overpowering sounds of celebration. Champagne and beer were flowing like water from a park fountain. Brit and Jeff had discussed the availability of beer and champagne for the event even though Donald never drank alcohol, smoked or condoned the use of those products. They realized that an event of this nature would require their availability to keep the crowd pumped up. It was expected. A lot of those in the room were grass roots supporters who had flown in from all over the country to enjoy this moment of victory they considered the most important event in modern US history. Others were there because they had invested their future in this town and its main industry, bureaucracy. If Donald Trump was the new sheriff in town, they wanted to be in his posse. The best road to success in Washington, D.C. was to be on the side of the winner. That's where the jobs were and the money would be spent. Many had supported both sides. Politicians and their respective parties come and go every four to eight years, but bureaucrats stay. If they wanted to retire with a large government pension, they couldn't care less who they called their boss. Blue-collar workers, truck drivers, Washington power brokers and diamond-encrusted socialites all stood tightly packed together waiting for Donald Trump to make his appearance. They understood fully that across town their counterparts on the losing side would be conducting a wake, not a victory party. They had chosen a winner and they fully intended to share in the perks and benefits of being on the right side of history. Eavesdropping on individuals throughout the great hall, one could make out a broad array of comments. You'd hear everything from, "He's our last chance to save this country" to "I don't really care for the man, but he will be running this town for next few years so we might as well make the best of the situation." There were as many different reasons for being there as there were guests. This odd mix of laborers and socialites was likely the most diverse group ever to celebrate a presidential election in the nation's capital.

By nine o'clock that evening, the festive mood of the event had ramped up due to the crowd's alcohol intake. Abruptly in mid-song, the band stopped playing a southern rock song as the lights dimmed in the ballroom. Andre Whittal walked out from behind the edge of a burgundy velvet curtain which had been opened wide revealing a section of bleacher-like seats centered on the stage behind a wooden podium bearing the Mayflower Hotel emblem. He fumbled with the microphone, unable to get it to function until a stagehand came forward and showed him the switch. It cut on with a large squawk over the PA system. The crowd quieted slowly. Andre waited until it was perfectly quiet in the room. The few audience members who didn't want to interrupt themselves even to hear the speaker were eventually quieted by whispers of 'hush' from those around them.

"Friends, supporters, staff members, associates, members of the media, and special guests. Today was a huge day for America. After being ignored for decades, the silent majority came alive and picked someone to champion their causes. This is a day of victory, a day of revitalization of the country and a day of celebrations. No one is more thrilled than I am but I know you didn't come here to listen to me. So, without further delay, I want to take this opportunity to introduce to you all, the man who needs no introduction. Donald Trump, the next President of the United States!"

The band started playing their own rock version of Hail to the Chief. The audience rolled with applause, shouts, hollers and whistles as Donald walked out on the stage with Melania followed by all of his children, their spouses and his grandchildren. Donald raised both arms in triumph as he approached the podium. Amid the thunderous roar, he mouthed "thank you, thank you, thank you."

The crowd went on with their applause for a full two minutes. On his third try to address them, the audience finally began to settle down. With the exception of a few undercurrents of small talk and the coughs of those who had just screamed to excess, the room once again grew quiet. Donald looked resplendent in his tailored, dark blue suit and presidential red tie. The oversized diamond-filled monogrammed cuff links sparkled as he raised his hands and thanked everyone.

"There are no words I could use here this evening to truly express my gratitude to all of you. Not just for being here tonight to help us celebrate, that's the easy part. No, I want to especially thank those of you who gave of your valuable time and energy to work in our regional offices throughout the country. You worked without pay, handing out leaflets, working our phone banks and just getting out there and talking to people about who we are, who I am, and what we want to do for our country. You did the hard work. You brought out the crowds when we visited your cities. You were tireless and unrelenting in your efforts. Without you, I wouldn't be here this evening. Now, there are many individuals I want to personally thank who are up here on the stage with me, but, and this is important; there are two things I know you and I have been waiting a long time to hear. So, I'll tell you right now. About an hour ago, Hillary Clinton called me and graciously conceded that we had won the election."

The crowd again burst into applause and screams that continued for over a full minute. Once they settled back down Donald continued. "So, with her concession, I can tell you without any further delay, I will be your next President of the United States."

Another round of applause and shouts spread across the massive ballroom, continuing unabated for two full minutes. Donald stood behind the podium. Melania had now come over to him and hugged him while the crowd cheered. When order was finally restored in the room, Donald continued his impromptu speech, using no notes or a teleprompter. He preferred to speak directly from his thoughts to his listener's' ears. Even if you did not agree with the message, you had to respect his method of speaking his own unrehearsed thoughts and core beliefs.

"We have just a few months left before we restore dignity and integrity to the office of the President. There will be no more veterans dying, waiting for medical help while V.A. directors lie about it. Under my watch, no director of the Internal Revenue Service will ever take the Fifth Amendment rather than tell the truth about their actions. We will not live in fear of small ruthless dictators who blow up women and children in shopping malls because our government is too paralyzed with political correctness to take any action."

Another full minute of applause burst out from the crowd at the mention of ending political correctness. Donald started again.

"No more will our Attorney General decide which laws he or she will and will not enforce. Nor will that office encourage any branch of government to withhold emails, documents, or information of any sort from government watchdogs. In my administration, whistleblowers will be celebrated, not persecuted or fired. I will never work around Congress and the courts by writing executive actions to circumvent the law. And here's a message for General Motors, AIG and JP Morgan: if you go bankrupt, no taxpayer money will be forthcoming to bail you out. That's a promise. I will build back our alliances with countries that used to trust us, before we abandoned them. I'll make certain that we are not on the losing end of every treaty and deal we undertake. Your healthcare will be your business, yours and your doctor's. Not the federal government's. Finally, I will never, ever make an apology tour to the rest of the world for anything this country has done over the past two hundred forty-one years. America will be great once again! I promise you all of this, with God as my witness."

The band started up again as Melania and the rest of the family, along with Donald's closest allies on the stage, all held hands and raised them above their heads in a victory salute to the huge crowd. The roar of approval lasted a full five minutes. When the mob of supporters quieted down again, Donald continued with his speech.

"I'd like to take just a moment to give thanks to some very special people here tonight. First, I think most of you heard of the tragic accident involving Jeremy Eason. He was one of our staffers, a volunteer. Jeremy had just graduated from college with a degree in Political Science. He was interested in government and all of its inner workings. This past fall, he was driving the tour bus we used on the campaign trail and died in a horrible accident. All of us who knew him were heartbroken. His mother, Betty Eason, is here with us tonight. Come over here, Betty, so we can recognize you and honor Jeremy."

She crossed the stage, stopping to get a hug from Melania and then another from Donald. She was too upset to speak and just raised her hand to the crowd who gave her a grateful round of applause.

"Thank you, Betty. And thank you for raising your son Jeremy to be such a very special young man. And now, let's bring a few more folks up here we need to recognize."

Over the next fifteen minutes, a series of special guests were recognized. When all the acknowledgements had been made, Donald spoke once more.

"And a special thanks to all of you out there this evening. Without your support, we certainly wouldn't be here tonight. Melania and I are excited to start making arrangements for our move into our new residence, the White House, and begin to right the course of America. Now, let's get on with the party. Melania and I will be here all evening with you. Please come by and say hello. There's plenty of food and champagne, so enjoy."

The Trumps had one of the best-known names in America. It resided on the fronts of many of the most notable buildings in the country. From New York City to Los Angeles to West Palm Beach, the name was prominently displayed on some of the most valuable real estate in the country. Over the past decade, the brand had spread out across the globe like a tidal wave. To reside in a Trump community or vacation in a Trump resort, meant you had achieved the American Dream from the standpoint of personal wealth and success. These were not properties where the working class could even think about owning or visiting. Donald was a natural with the media. He relished the attention and had an innate aptitude for dealing with it. Never shy, he relished time in front of the cameras and used every instance of the attention to promote his investments and his name. The name Trump was now synonymous with wealth. His opinions, influence, and presence were sought after by anyone and everyone. To know him, was a huge plus in the business world. To be able to get him on the phone or an invitation to his office, meant you were traveling in the highest orbit. He and Melania circulated around the dance floor in The Mayflower's large ballroom. He knew almost everyone there. Those whose faces he couldn't associate with a name, got a hug, a handshake, or smile and a gracious "how wonderful to see you here" as if they were the best of friends. When it came to playing these games, he was the king. With his aristocratic bearing and alongside his beautiful wife, a former model, they made a striking couple. They were both used to the limelight. Being the center of attention only heightened their ability to own a room. By midnight he was spent. Though you'd never know it by his face or outward movements. It had been a long day at the end of a long year on the campaign trail. He knew that unless someone had actually been through it, they couldn't begin to even visualize just how grueling it was. That part of winning the office was not what he preferred, but he had understood it was the process he'd have to go through to get it done. Thank God it was over. Spending a few weeks traveling less and getting his cabinet in place would be invigorating. That's where he was ready to focus for the immediate future. He'd made a lot of promises along the way, and he intended to deliver on every one of them. Standing in Donald Trump's way had never been a good idea for any of those who had tried it. He wasn't a mean person, but he was driven. If someone got in his way, well that was their problem. Andre Whittal approached Donald and Melania as they started to leave the grand ballroom and head up to their suite.

"This go as you thought it would, sir?"

"Never 'sir' when it's just us, Andre. In the Oval Office, it might be appropriate, but socially I'm just Donald. Got it?"

"I do, sir, I mean Donald. Do you want to say anything else to the crowd before you leave for the night?"

"No, I think it's best to leave things right where they are for now. I think everyone is enjoying the celebration, full of hope for the future, and they're excited about what this all means for the country."

"To tell you the truth, sir, no one is more excited about it than me."

"I'm right there with you, Andre. Now, let's all go get some well-earned rest. I feel like I need to sleep for about a week."

Donald and Melania exited the elevator accompanied by two Secret Service agents who walked them over to the door of their suite. Another young man holding a small radio greeted them. The two agents addressed Donald and Melania and assured them the suite was clean and safe for the night. The senior of the three agents spoke directly to Donald.

"Sir, the room is clear. This is the only entry point and we swept the rooms inside again just a short while ago. I hope you and Mrs. Trump have a quiet and restful evening. There will be agents just outside the door throughout the night if you need anything, and that means anything."

"That's fine, young man. What is your name?"

"Christian Baylor, sir."

"And what do your friends call you?"

"Chris, sir."

"And you'll be part of the team I'll have around me from here on out?"

"I don't know for how long, sir. But for now, that's correct."

"Well, Chris, Melania had mentioned how gracious you were to her all afternoon and if it's all right with you, I'm going to request that you be given the assignment of being with us full-time. Would you be OK with that?"

"I'd be honored, sir."

"I'll get on that request in the morning. Chris, have a good night yourself. Get some rest. We have a busy time ahead of us."

"Yes, sir. See you tomorrow."

Donald and Melania entered the room and closed the door behind them.

"Finally, it's down to just you and me. When it's all been said and done, these are the times that are the most important, when you and I are alone together. You know, I have the best soul mate, wife and friend of anyone on the planet. And, she just happens to be a very sexy woman."

"You are a mess, Donald. If we weren't both completely exhausted I'd swear you were trying to come on to me."

"Maybe not tonight, though the thought did cross my mind earlier, I will admit. For the first time in over a year, I really don't have any appointments tomorrow until after lunch. I'm thinking about sleeping in, having a decadent breakfast in bed, and then giving you a couple of hours of the kind of undivided attention you deserve."

"Well now, Mr. President, I've heard you don't make any promises you don't intend to keep."

"That is the word on the street about me."

"I've heard, I've heard. I'm anxious to see just how true those rumors are."

4

January 20, 2017- Inauguration Day

Donald and Andre were carefully examining the Oval Office just hours after he had been sworn in as President.

"So, we're here. We made it. No one could possibly imagine the amount of effort, perseverance and gut-churning it took."

"Yes, sir. It's not for the faint of heart or the thin-skinned. Before it was over with, I never wanted to strangle so many people so much in my entire life."

"What do they say, Andre? Politics is a blood sport. You better believe it. You just have to ignore the naysayers and move on. Remember, they don't personally dislike me. That's not it at all. They just want to be here themselves and they'll say or do anything to make it happen. Power can be the most addicting of all aphrodisiacs."

Donald walked around the room, stopping to admire each painting and piece of furniture.

"The room looks just like I remembered it."

"You've been in here before?"

"Yes, I had the pleasure under several previous Presidents. You give them enough campaign contributions and bingo, you get the invite. Interesting enough, I've been here under both Republican and Democratic Presidents. It's funny, but cash has no party affiliation. Enough small talk. Let's get our folks in here, give them the quick tour, get that behind us, and get to work. Tell Greta to gather them up and let's do this in about thirty minutes."

"Done."

Andre walked out of the office and over to the new presidential secretary, Greta Mossburg.

"Greta, the President would like all of his staff that are available to come into his office in thirty minutes for a quick meeting and to look around so they can get that out of their system. I have a feeling that it's going to get busy around here very quickly."

"Yes, sir. Thirty minutes it is."

In short order, fifteen of Donald's closest advisors and staff gathered in the Oval Office. Prior to the election, he had known most of them for years and the majority had worked for him previously in some capacity. They had proven to be not only trustworthy, but the best and the brightest in their fields. None had previous government experience yet they all shared Donald's general impression that government employees had been the problem and not the cure for the past fifty years.

"Good afternoon everyone. I wanted to share this moment with you all since none of us would be here if you had not given one hundred ten percent of your best effort to make this happen. I know what you're all capable of and that's why I've brought you along on this journey. Things in Washington, in the government, have been headed in the wrong direction for a long time and right now a lot of things have reached critical mass. Most government workers don't understand free enterprise and most of them hold it in contempt. They're working in a cocoon of such limited exposure that they're unable to connect the dots and see that without free enterprise and the dollars it generates, there would be no government and they'd all be out of work. The average hard-working people in this country understood it very clearly and sent us here to clean up this mess. There is going to be a lot of resistance. Washington has been a gravy train for a long time for these people, and they are not going to give it up without a fight. You saw how it was during the campaign. Multiply that by a thousand and you'll have what's going to be happening here. I'm up to it, and I know you are too. I want you to see the worth in what you're doing and not think of yourselves as slaves. Yes, there' are going to be some incredibly long days and a lot of frustration, but I want you to enjoy what you do. If you have problems, I'm here. Just like it was back in New York, my door is always open. Tell me or Andre about the problems before they grow larger. I don't want anything happening that I'm not informed about. We'll have a staff meeting every morning. Some of you will be in those meetings. The rest of you will be steering the ship while we discuss the course. So, let's all pull together and make this happen. Take a few minutes while you're here to look around the Oval Office. There's a lot of history here. Most Americans will never get the opportunity to be inside the Oval Office, even though their sweat and blood built it. Respect what it means and remember who we work for."

Donald walked over to Andre and spoke quietly as the staff perused their surroundings.

"Day one. What do you think should be job one?"

"That's your call, sir. I'll put in motion whatever you think we need to get started on."

"Let's get the staff list out first and see what positions we need to be looking at for replacements. I'd also like a list of every possible appointment I'm authorized to make, which jobs come under my personal discretion. Let's have someone from the Capitol Police come by and talk to me about how security works around here. I want to keep some of my own security staff involved. I've dealt with them a long time and they're top notch. I'd like them to be a part of whatever is done, even if they're just monitoring. And one other thing I'm particularly anxious to work on."

"Yes, sir?"

"I want the names of every one of those so-called czars that were appointed by my predecessor to circumvent Congress and the law. I want them out of my administration before the sun goes down. Got it?"

"I don't know what took you so long."

"We'll be doing a lot of house cleaning this week."

Andre left the room and Donald sat down behind the grand, historic *Resolute* desk that was centered in the room. Now that he had the room to himself, he looked around at the portraits of some of his predecessors and took in the significance of where he was and what he was undertaking. He opened his black book and starting considering the names of those that he thought might be an asset on his staff. He knew a great many accomplished people, but he understood there is a lot of difference between government service and free enterprise. Some business elites wouldn't have the stomach to deal with the basic feeling of entitlement that permeated Washington. The day passed quickly. Staff members, trying to get their feet on the ground, understand exactly what their parameters were and what their focus should be, called on Donald throughout the afternoon. It was how he did business, and he was pleased to see his trusted allies bringing an order he understood to his new office.

A little after eight p.m., Greta called Donald on his private intercom. "Mr. President, may I come see you a moment?"

Donald was a little surprised that she would call while he was taking a meeting with several staff members but realized it must be of some significance.

"Come on in, Greta."

The slightly bent, silver-haired Greta walked into the Oval office. She wore her glasses low on her nose so she could see better as she walked. Her outstretched hand passed an index card to Donald. She explained the name on the card as he took it.

"I just received a call from a young Army officer, a Lieutenant Drexler. His name's on the bottom of that card. He said that General Morrison wants to see you tonight. He's the Chairman of the Joint Chiefs of Staff."

"He needs to see me tonight? Are we under attack?"

"He didn't say what the urgency was, only that it was crucial that he meet with you this evening before you left the office. What would you like me to tell him?"

"I'm already starting to wear down a little, but I don't want to start off on a bad foot with the military. I was planning on meeting with them this week anyway, so I guess a short chat this evening might be a good introduction prior to that meeting. Greta, tell him to come over as soon as he can get here. I'm anxious to get back to Melania. I promised her we'd make time to be with each other every day, and I want to honor that promise especially on my first day in office."

"I understand, sir. I'll get back with them right away."

In less than ten minutes, the intercom from Greta's desk buzzed in again.

"Yes, Greta."

"General Morrison is here."

"Really, he must have been in the parking lot when he called you to set this up. I'm available right now. Escort him in please."

"Sir, he says that he wants to meet in the Situation Room as it's more appropriate for your discussion tonight."

"I guess that's all right with me. I can't imagine why he doesn't want to meet in my office, but let's keep the general happy. Greta. Do you know how to get there from here?"

"Yes, sir. I've learned the layout of the place down pretty well. Do you want me to escort you there?"

"You probably need to. Andre and I will both meet with him. I want Andre to know these folks as well as I do, so he can handle some of these meetings in the future."

Donald noticed as they walked through the reception room and out to the hall that there were young men and women within eyesight at all times. They always appeared razor sharp and the look unmistakably Secret Service. They wore business suits but to Donald they looked like a cross between Wall Street interns and someone in basic training. As the three walked past, they quietly spoke into lapel microphones to let the next agent along the way know that Donald, who they referred to as Mogul, was on the move. He didn't really know why they chose that nickname and hoped it wasn't derogatory to denote he was coming from the business world into their kingdom. He'd think about asking them to change it after a few days. Greta showed him down the hall past a number of closed doors to a set of double doors with an agent standing guard. They were quickly approaching the intelligence management hub located in the basement of the West Wing, formally known as the John F. Kennedy Conference Room. Just as they arrived at The Situation Room, the agent opened the door while he greeted the President.

"Good evening, Mr. President, Mr. Whittal."

"Good evening to you, young man."

As they entered the room, he was somewhat surprised to see four uniformed officers sitting near the end of a long conference table. The room was just as he had seen it in photos. The walls were covered with television screens, computer monitors, charts, and white boards. His own portrait now hung in a frame close to the entrance. It was surprising how quickly things had changed to reflect the presence of a new Commander-in-Chief. The officers all stood at attention as Donald entered. The oldest man among them walked briskly over to him. The silver stars on his shoulders and chest full of medals clearly showed he was the senior officer in the room. He stretched out his hand and gave Donald a strong handshake.

"Mr. President, it's an honor to meet you."

"The same to you. General Morrison?"

"That's correct. I'm Claiborne Morrison. I'm serving as Chairman of the Joint Chiefs of Staff."

"Four stars, eh? That would make you a Lieutenant General?"

"No, sir. That would make me a General. Lieutenant General is three stars."

"Very good, general. 'Thank you for your many years of outstanding service to your country."

Donald looked over to the younger officers and nodded.

"And to you gentlemen, thank you. Let me introduce my Chief of Staff, Andre Whittal."

Andre shook the general's hand as well and nodded toward the younger officers.

The general walked back to his seat at the end of the table and pointed to the two seats closest to him on the opposite side of the table from his staff.

"You might want to be seated, sir. This will take a few minutes."

Donald and Andre were both taken aback by the general more or less directing them to take a seat. Whether the President, the Commander-in-Chief and his direct superior wanted to sit or not sit was clearly not his concern. Rather than start the meeting off on a bad note, Donald and Andre each pulled out a chair and sat down across from the general's staff.

"I assume this must be of some importance, general, not being able to wait a few days until we got settled into our offices."

"After this meeting, I'm sure you'll agree that it was best not to put it off."

"OK. I'm all yours. What's on your mind, General Morrison?"

"First, let me give you a little history on this meeting. The Chiefs of Staff have been having this same meeting with each incoming President for over sixty years."

"Really? It's something I didn't know about."

Donald smiled as he continued. "I guess there's probably a lot of little surprises I'll hear about in the coming weeks. I particularly have some questions about UFOs, but that can wait until another time."

The general continued though he wasn't amused by Donald's lack of complete attention.

"It will have to. Now as I was saying, this has been a long-standing arrangement and this meeting is critical to help you understand the relationship the President has with our armed forces. First, let me ask you a question."

"What pulled the United States out of the Great Depression?"

"Most scholars would say it was World War II."

"They would be correct. America was dying. At the end of World War I, the country was booming. It was The Roaring Twenties. The stock market was out of control. People were getting ahead. There was optimism everywhere. Slowly, after the war, the government quit spending on the military. It depended on the purchasing power of the general public. Over time, it slowed and the economy started to falter. In 1929, the overpriced stock market crashed. As a result, the world economy tanked. Millions were out of work. The country had no central purpose, no national goal. And then World War II started. Trust me, a lot of things had to happen in just the right order to have the entire world involved in the war. The nation banded together to stop Germany and Japan from taking over the world. We went from a bare bones defense system with limited capabilities to the most powerful military on Earth in just a couple of years. With the future of the world depending on us, the U.S. started spending whatever it took to build up the military. Suddenly, everybody who wanted a job had one. Millions of depressed, unemployed young men joined the military. Nobody was worried about the economy. By the end of the war, America was booming again. President Coolidge said, 'The chief business of the American people is business'. That's not correct. The chief business of the American people is war. Since World War II, the world has grown much smaller. Trouble in the world anywhere has an effect on every other nation, some to a larger degree than others. The 24/7 news media ensures that an uprising in the morning in Kenya is on the evening news worldwide with live video. Trade is affected. People are uprooted and emigrate to other countries. Alliances between world powers are tested daily. Any country in the world is only an airplane ride away from having a terrorist bomb go off in a shopping mall or an elementary school. In that regard, the world is very dangerous. There's really not much an army, an air force, two hundred thousand soldiers or an aircraft carrier can do to stop two or three individuals in some town say, for example, Oklahoma City, from setting off a bomb they made themselves and killing many innocent people. It's going on all over the world as we speak. Governments are almost helpless against it. That's especially true here in the States where some strung-out bunch of politically correct wackos don't want anybody profiled, monitored, investigated or even punished when they're caught. It's a very difficult time we live in."

Donald was growing impatient. "I'm aware of all that you're saying, but we need to get to the point as it's getting late."

"Yes, it certainly is. OK, I'll be more blunt."

"The Presidency is not what it used to be. It has become more of a figurehead type of position, like the Queen of England. The power in America no longer depends on the transitory and short-lived ideas of a single person. The power lies now where it should, with the people who actually keep the country safe. By that, I mean the military."

"What are you talking about? You sound like someone out of Dr. Strangelove. I'm not amused by what you're saying."

"That's good because I'm not saying these things to amuse you. I'm sure they're upsetting you. You ran on a platform of bringing major change and reforming government. That all sounds good, but the fact is that you're not in a position to change anything.

We've had many Presidents before you. Some very wealthy and powerful, just as you are. Kennedy, for example. Initially, Vietnam was a cause he favored. He believed in the domino effect. If the communists gained a foothold in Vietnam, it would lead to more governments falling to them. He agreed that it had to be stopped. Things were going along well. When the war became unpopular at home, thanks to the bleeding hearts in the media, he began to have second thoughts. He even enlisted the CIA to help assassinate a few folks over there to turn the tide. If he had just listened to us, and kept the hell out of the day-to-day affairs of the war, we could have taken care of everything and kept the country on course. Vietnam was a war just when we needed one. The U.S. started upgrading its defense, building some more jets and aircraft carriers. But Kennedy was turning against us, so we suggested he take a ride in a parade. Then Johnson was in office. He was a hawk, and we felt he could handle it. Again, the media and a weak stomach. We had to ask him to get out of the Presidency, so he agreed to not run for re-election. After all that drama, we've had to tighten up our day-to-day management of the Presidency. It's better for the country to not have a political maverick in here every few years thinking they know how to run the world. They don't. We do. You need to understand, this is not my organization. I'm just a soldier, a hired hand, if you will. I'm given orders, and I follow them just like every responsible general before me. I work for a small and brilliant group of individuals who have a very good understanding of the world situation and how it all fits together. They possess an expansive global view that encompasses much more than someone like you would have as the leader of just one country. You were elected by a bunch of uninformed people that don't see anything other than their house, the road they live on, their family unit and their own little paychecks. They elected you to look out for them, not the world. I will congratulate you on your victory though. We spent hundreds of millions trying to keep you from getting elected and having to deal with what you are finding out right now. We would rather have had one of our own elected to your position. So now, you're their employee and you'll do exactly what they tell you to do. I try to do what I'm told by the people who gave me this job. No difference, really."

"You are very wrong in your assumption, General. My election was the result of the people of this country coming to realize that something was dramatically wrong in Washington. Obviously, they were correct. For that reason alone, you will be removed unceremoniously from your post in short order. You and the traitors you are working with. You can count on that."

"I don't doubt your sincerity, Donald, but you couldn't be further from reality. Things are actually going quite well. We've got the Middle East. What a stroke of genius that place is. They've been at war over there for thousands of years. It's all they know. And the great news is it's sitting on top of billions of barrels of oil. That gives every western country a great interest in having input in how they run their sand-filled hellholes over there. Thus, a permanent war. It's been fifteen years now and it's still going strong. Presidents can't stop it. Nobody can. There're more damn warring factions over there than existed on the entire planet during both World Wars. It's the perfect scenario."

By this time, Andre was seething at the general's disrespect and demeanor toward Donald.

"You don't know what you're talking about, General. You're ruining your career at this very moment. You need to go back to the Pentagon and put in your notice for early retirement first thing in the morning. Your time on the Joint Chiefs just ended."

"And you, sir, need to sit back down and listen, whatever you said your name was. You aren't a player here. It was a mistake for Donald to even bring you with him to this meeting. He basically put you in harm's way by letting you come along."

Donald stood up, obviously fuming. "This is outrageous! This meeting is over."

He walked over to the door, opened it and turned to the two Secret Service agents standing just outside the door. He directed them.

"You men come in here and escort the general and his staff off the grounds."

The two men stepped inside The Situation Room and closed the door behind them. Without speaking, they directed their attention to the general. He then motioned for them to leave the room as he said to them, "Please go back to your stations. The President is, well, having a moment, you might say. Go back to your posts and I'll let you know if you're needed."

"Yes, sir."

With a growing air of authority General Morrison continued. "As you can see, contrary to what I'm certain you were thinking, you are not in any way in charge here. You will quickly discern that I, and the people I work with, run every inch of the White House and for that matter the Capitol and the country."

Again, an impatient Andre jumped up. "I'm leaving. Donald, I'll get this handled. General, you and your little collection of idiots better be gone before I get back."

The general looked over to one of the agents behind Andre and nodded. The agent immediately withdrew a semi-automatic pistol from a shoulder holster hidden under his suit coat. Before Andre could take three steps toward the door, the young agent smashed the butt of the pistol into the back of his skull. It wasn't a glancing blow designed only to render him unconscious and defenseless. It was a skull-shattering blow that dropped Andre so quickly he never even winced or groaned. As Andre fell to the floor, Donald was frozen in place by the violence he'd just witnessed. There was a slight gurgling sound coming from the throat of his lifelong friend lying motionless on the floor. A small stream of blood trickled from his mouth onto the floor. In just a few seconds, there was total silence. Two other agents joined Andre's assailant as they picked up the lifeless body and carried it from the room.

Unfazed, as if nothing had occurred, General Morrison continued, "I always hate it when we have to make an example so early in our relationship with a new President. Oh, don't think your man there was the first person to go through this in The Situation Room. At some point, the human spirit will fight the inevitable and then, well, you saw for yourself. Now sit back down and pay attention to what I'm saying. I won't be coming back here to go through this again."

Donald was dumbfounded. Part of him wanted to get up and run from the room, but the opposite side of his brain told him it would be best to let the maniac finish his speech, appear to comply, and engineer a plan of retaliation as quickly as possible once he left.

"You know I have no choice but to hear you out. I've just witnessed you murder Andre Whittal, a man I've known over thirty years and trusted with my very life. I completely understand that you're capable of killing innocent people in a heartbeat. So, go ahead. Enlighten me as to what you're doing here."

"Good, I hope we can continue peacefully now. I don't like violence any more than anyone else, though I'm certain I've seen a lot more than most. Let's talk a little more history for a moment. After World War II, it was apparent to a handful of very smart and powerful people that everything had changed. For the first time a single nation, just one leader, could start something that could destroy the planet, kill everyone living on it. The bombs dropped at Nagasaki and Hiroshima were tiny, just a quarter of a megaton. Today, many countries possess weapons containing multiple warheads of over a hundred megatons each. Any skirmish blown out of control could result in a barrage of these weapons being used and thus the end of civilization, as we know it. So an organization was started, run by these same powerful men, most of who are not from any specific government. They are more or less concerned citizens of the world. They went over every possible scenario of what could happen and the steps they would take to prevent a worldwide catastrophe. You see, despite the fact that occasionally someone has to leave this world early, like your friend Andre, these are men of peace and compassion trying their best to prevent the death of billions of people and the end of life on Earth. There is no more noble cause than that."

Donald remained motionless with no expression on his face. He stared at the general as he continued.

"A few principals in our organization are just as prominent in the business world as you have been. That's where most of our members come from. They understood there were a few nations in a much better position than others to engineer the peace, to steer the world in a positive direction. Now, as we all know there are small wars going on all the time. The United States has been involved in a number of them. It's human nature to go to war, to kill your enemies. It's actually good for the world economy. The armies and navies of many countries spend untold billions of dollars every year trying to make sure they're able to win in the event they are attacked. Some, with juvenile dictators like the maniac in North Korea, are stupid enough to think they could actually win a war against a major power. The truth is we have the ability to explode their missiles while they are still in their silos. Their navies could be rusty, man-made reefs in seconds if our organization determined that's what needed to happen. So, it was necessary to gain control of the governments of a few major powers. The United States was the dominant country at the end of World War II, so this was the most logical place to start. The military was incredibly strong and held in high regard by our citizens. Some other federal organizations were coming into prominence as well, such as the FBI and the Secret Service. We consolidated all of these institutions under one umbrella controlled by our organization. There were those who stupidly tried to prevent this from happening, people like your friend Andre. One person, two, ten or ten thousand are not even relevant when compared to maintaining peace and order throughout the world. It's sometimes referred to as 'the greater good.' So that's where we came from and how this all started. Over the years, our organization has increased its control throughout many nations. We control all branches of the government here. With the explosion of technology, our job has become increasingly easier. We have eyes on just about everyone and everything. The Capitol is literally wired from one end to the other. And in what is probably the most ironic part of all this effort, the people that you might think are there to look out for you, are actually working for us. With every move you make, there are agents with you. You will have the Secret Service 'protecting' you and your family for life. That's many years after you leave here. Wherever you go, wherever your wife, your kids, even your dog goes, we're there. We watch what you do, listen to what you say. There's really nowhere you can go to undo what we have going here, no one to tell this to, no one you can try to convince to help you come after us. We control them all.

One of the lower-ranked officers approached the general from behind.

"General, I'm sorry to interrupt. It's coming on right now."

Morrison pointed to a large television monitor on the wall. He smirked as he spoke. "For example, let's see what's happening right now on the news." He pointed to the screen as he ordered a soldier closest to the set, "Lieutenant Drexler, let's turn the volume up for the President."

CNN was just starting to cover an event that disturbed Donald even more than what had just occurred in The Situation Room. A reporter was near an overpass within the capital. Along the bottom of the screen, the words 'Breaking News' scrolled continuously.

"We are here just off the Beltway headed toward Fairfax. You can see the black SUV down the embankment, still smoldering. Eyewitnesses said it appears Mr. Whittal lost control of his vehicle just before the exit and it plunged over the rail, bursting into flames on impact. An off-duty Capitol Police Sergeant who was headed home at the end of his shift tried unsuccessfully to pull President Trump's new Chief of Staff from the overturned car. He indicated that Mr. Whittal appeared unconscious behind the wheel. The flames quickly spread and the Sergeant was unable to free him from the wrecked car before the flames engulfed the passenger area. A very tragic beginning to President Trump's first day in office. Back to you, Martin."

Coverage then returned to the news anchor at the main network studio.

"There's no word from the White House yet, but we are told that a statement will be forthcoming very soon. A very sad day indeed. We'll have much more on this breaking story as it unfolds. Later tonight, we'll have a special report detailing the career of Andre Whittal, an accomplished attorney and long-time personal friend of President Trump."

The general directed the young officer to turn off the television.

"That's enough. As you can see, Donald it's not hard for us to engineer what happens here with flawless attention to detail. The media is a large part of what we do. It's not only important to control what actually goes on in the world, but also to control the public's perception of it. You might be shocked to realize how dumb the public actually is. Of course, we like to use the term 'uninformed.' The men and women that fought in Europe and Japan and today are buried in national cemeteries all over the world would roll over in their graves if they could see what a weak nation of mindless, unconcerned children we've raised. Getting control of education was huge in our plan. You could call it a dagger in the heart of common sense. And let's not overlook our biggest ally, political correctness. That was the final piece of the puzzle. Today's citizens, for the most part are more concerned about how things appear, than how they actually are. Let's not hurt anyone's feelings, shall we? Sometimes I can't believe it myself. In less than four generations, we've created the most pathetic group of robots that ever lived. Thank God they're not in control of anything except the channel on their television set. We're very good at what we do. So, where are we now? Let's talk about what's expected from you."

By now, Donald was weak and drained. This had come out of nowhere. It was much worse than anything he could have ever dreamed could occur. He sat motionless as the general continued to pontificate.

"Like quite a few Presidents before you, you are a large part of what we do, like it or not. Every day you will receive a manila folder from us. It will contain in detail our current and long-term initiatives. We will be directing your travel, your press conferences, any contact with the public or with individuals and organizations. Your speeches will be written by us and always directed for you via teleprompter. I know you loved to brag that you speak from the heart and off the cuff, never with a teleprompter. You certainly bad-mouthed your predecessor for using one. But, it wasn't his choice; it was ours. We can't take the chance that you'll remember all that we want you talk about and use the exact words chosen to express our views. We'll dictate them to you exactly as we want them said. You will not deviate from them. If the teleprompter goes down for any reason, and that's a rare occurrence, you can talk about the weather, the Super Bowl, your kids, whatever meaningless things you want to, but never about anything of significance. I want to be very clear about that. We dictate everything of a policy nature or an initiative you present to the public. All of your travel plans go through us, where you visit, the other world leaders you meet with. Trust me, any leader of another major power is operating under the same set of parameters that you will be. If they don't go along with the program... Well, you've seen the consequences. Any attempt by you to circumvent our control, any effort to tell the public at large or enlist any resistance, we will immediately respond to it as an act of treason. This has been going on for a long time. There have been several before you who mistakenly thought they could retake the power from us. That didn't go too well for them. There have been others who lost the public's support when they were discovered doing some pretty disgusting things, even in the Oval Office. Some have lost all credibility and, even in a rare occurrence, met with an untimely end such as the aforementioned parade in Dallas. Remember, nothing here happens by accident. We're everywhere you are from here on out. And that includes your family. We're in your office, your car, every place you go all day, even in your bedroom. And by the way, your own security staff is out of here, one hundred percent. You will do what we want, when we want. We don't expect any violations of these rules. We are the government of all nations and you are just a short-term figurehead, someone for the public to gawk at to make them feel secure in their belief that they choose who runs things. It's just not how it is. I do appreciate your meeting with me this evening after a long first day in office. My staff and I have other meetings yet this evening, late as it is. I'll leave you to your thoughts. Those can still be whatever you want, as long as you keep them to yourself. Good evening, Mr. President."

With that, General Morrison stood up, motioned with his hand for his staff to leave the room. Several agents left the room. The younger officers followed the general. For a few moments, Donald remained in the room to assimilate in his mind the horrific events that had just unfolded.

✶ ✶ ✶

In a deep state of depression coupled with an anxiety he'd never known, Donald entered the private bedroom in the White House. Melania was smiling as he entered.

"Good evening, Mr. President."

Completely distracted, he walked over to the closet taking his jacket off as he walked. He stared absent-mindedly at the tie rack as he took off the custom silk tie he had been wearing.

"Donald? What on earth are you thinking about? You walked past me as if I weren't here."

"I'm sorry. I've had a very difficult day. Have you been listening to the news?"

"No, not this evening. What happened?"

"Andre is dead. A terrible car wreck not far from the Capitol, on the Beltway."

"My God! I hadn't heard anything. Does Sandra know?"

"I'm not sure. It's late, but we should call her. I'll make the call and see what she knows. Then you can speak with her. I really don't feel all that well right now."

Donald picked up the receiver in the room and the ever-present White House operator immediately placed the call. Andre's wife Sandra answered. Donald knew from the sound of her voice that she already knew the terrible news. He would never tell her the full truth about what occurred.

"Sandra, I'm so very sorry. He had just left the White House. I got word ten minutes later of the crash. We're here for you. If there is anything we can do, me or Melania, we will gladly do it. Here's Melania."

Melania took the phone. As she and Sandra talked, Donald went to the bathroom. He looked at his image in the mirror and could barely believe how tired he looked. It had always been an interesting side note of Presidents to see pictures when they first took office and how much they had aged by the end of their terms. Donald felt as if his own reflection appeared to have aged considerably since just that morning. He couldn't help but think about what he had gotten involved with and its long-term effect on him and those he loved. If they would so easily kill Andre, there would be no limit to what they would do in order to protect the monumental conspiracy they had constructed. When Melania finished her phone call, they lay in bed together and talked about the day's unforeseeable events. Melania had always been a loving wife, his third. She was much younger than him, but a loving and considerate spouse.

"Donald, can you take off a few days and rest? You look terribly tired and losing your best friend has shaken you. I can see it in your eyes. Surely everything would be fine if you just took off a day or two. I know you want to help plan some sort of memorial event for Andre."

"I do. But, no. There's no way I can take a day off. There's more to be done here than I can possibly tell you. It's, it's not anything like I thought it would be. It's going to be a very difficult job. I really didn't understand how hard it would be. I guess nobody could really understand the enormous pressure of this job until you are actually there. Nothing can truly prepare you for it."

"You've always been in a very high-stress situation at work. You've always dealt with crises of one kind or another. Is this that different?"

"I met with a man this afternoon. A general. He is the Chairman of the Joint Chiefs of Staff. Basically, he runs the entire military complex of the country. A very powerful man. He..."

The phone across the room rang. Fearing that Sandra Whittal might be having a meltdown and needing her to come over to console her, Melania ran to the phone. She was more than surprised to hear a young male voice asking for Donald.

"It's a military officer of some sort. He says he needs to speak with you right now."

Donald was shocked by a call at this hour.

"Hello, this is Donald Trump."

"I'm sorry to bother you so late, Mr. President. I am in charge of the overnight monitoring bureau here in the Pentagon. I have to tell you that you need to drop the conversation with the First Lady about General Morrison or any other matter regarding the Executive Branch and military liaisons you have been made aware of. If at any time, you are heard to be exceeding your conversational limits, someone from this office will contact you. Night or day, 24/7. Sorry to disturb you, Mr. President, but it's my job. Goodnight, sir."

Donald dropped the phone back on the hook without a response. He turned to walk back over to the bed. Melania stared at him.

"Donald, you look like you've just seen a ghost. What was that all about?"

"Just an update on the wreck. Some of the members of the military were offering condolences. Nothing serious."

"Your face is telling me something different than what you are saying."

"I really can't discuss with you everything about being President that I'd like to. It's for your own protection. I'm sorry if I seem distant or less than candid. This is what I was telling you about a minute ago. Things are nothing like what I thought they would be. Nothing."

5

The extravagant penthouse gleamed with stainless steel, glass and polished mahogany throughout. General Morrison sat in a dark red, leather chair and listened intently. It was readily apparent from his body language and his forced smile that he was a subordinate to the man sitting behind the stately desk directly in front of him. This was far removed from his persona at the Pentagon. Never interrupting and constantly nodding, he more resembled a Boy Scout listening to his Troop Master than the Chairman of the Joint Chiefs of Staff. The person seated directly in front of him stared intently at Morrison as he spoke. The unquestioned air of his authority permeated the office. He was there to express his demands, not to listen or consider those of anyone else. His speech was deliberate, every word carefully chosen so there could be no mistake as to their meaning.

"Our leadership was not pleased by yet another death in The Situation Room. You seem to be making this a habit, Claiborne. Was this absolutely necessary?"

"Donald Trump is a very powerful man. He's not used to being told what to do by anyone. He was starting to push back. When his Chief of Staff tried to jump in between us and exert some clout, it was the only course of action to take. It was over in just seconds and Trump got the message. He became instantly more compliant after that. I'd say it was just the right move at a critical moment."

"That sounds almost verbatim to what you said last time. How about not resorting to violence from here on out? Certainly, there's already enough in this business to satisfy you."

"I see no need to take any additional actions in that direction. I'm certain Donald Trump will do exactly what we tell him from here on out."

"I hope you're correct in that regard. These damned elections every four years really get in the way of our day-to-day operations. I suppose they're necessary to keep the average idiot on the street believing they have a little say in what goes on around here. Thank God they don't. At least we got Snowden in as the V.P. How's that going? Did you tell Trump that Snowden was our guy?"

"I never even hinted at it. I do know that he's not thrilled that the party insisted he put him on the ticket. He's aware that Snowden isn't on his team but I don't think he has a clue that he's on ours. When the time comes, he'll do exactly what we want him to do."

"That sounds good. Look, I want you to bring Snowden over here later this week. Trump will be occupied with everything he's into, so he won't miss him. We have serious plans underway and I want Snowden to be prepared for what's in store for him. I don't like to leave anything to chance. What day can you have him here?"

"Let me get back with you later today. I'll get a specific time for the meeting."

"That'll work. Now, let's talk about the strategy we will execute over the next sixty days. How are things moving along in Yemen? Is everything in place? We don't want any action until the rebels have the weapons. That would be bad for business and send the wrong message. I mean, no weapons, no war. Isn't that so, General?"

"No question. I have personally seen drone videotapes of the weapons handoff. We have several contractors who've been schooling the rebels this past week on how the weapons function. Considering they have the IQ of a rabbit, they're about as ready as we need them to be. We've placed a couple of assets there to set off the initial blasts in four or five crowded public places. The rebels will take full credit, and the game will be on."

"It's critical that everyone who can be traced to elements from outside of Yemen be gone when this all goes down. It has to appear to be all locals with an axe to grind with their own government. No signs of any outside intervention. Just like Syria. Your people understand this fully?"

"Absolutely. We're using the same game plan as before. In ten days, the entire place will be a war zone."

"I want to know the minute the bombs go off. Get us some aerial footage from a drone and then be ready to field requests for help from President Hadi. You're aware that he and Trump know each other?"

"I do. They've had a relationship for some time and remained in touch over the years. That will work tremendously in our favor. He'll turn to his old friend for help, open their treasury, and call President Trump."

"The U.S. has an aid and assistance treaty in place with Yemen so they'll expect us to do whatever necessary to keep Hadi in power. Of course, we will do so while maintaining our friendship with and assistance to the rebels simultaneously. Always a pretty narrow tightrope to walk, but you have shown competence in managing these operations, Claiborne. That's why we have you. Now, one more thing about Trump. We don't think he's going to be as compliant as you seem to believe he will. He's not the usual political hack we have to work with, who're used to taking orders from whoever put up the money to buy the office for them. Trump made his own money and doesn't do a good job at taking orders. At some point, he's going to buck us. Count on it. He's smart enough to know we have the upper hand right now, but I assure you his brain is working overtime at this moment trying to figure out who we are and what he needs to do to get rid of us. That makes him dangerous. He' has to be monitored around the clock, and his family and close friends as well. We don't want anything to slip past us."

"You can count on that. We're on top of him and his family. Every move they make from brushing their teeth to taking a crap will be monitored, twenty four seven."

"Please, General, save your gutter talk for the barracks. We like to think of ourselves as civilized here. Trying to save society and remain on top of it is what we're all about. Let's try to stay on the high road, shall we?"

"Yes, sir. I was just using an expression."

"We both know the seriousness of what we are doing. We know the odds we face and the ramifications if anything should go wrong. These are high-stakes maneuvers. If you screw up or compromise any part of this operation, there will be a huge price to pay. You work with us, maintain discretion, and stay on top of what we ask you to do and the rewards are abundant, as you have already seen. Now, I have an envelope here for you to give to the President. You can wait for him to go over it and make sure he understands every word of our agenda. Then, make certain he's always on a teleprompter when he does appearances. We want no impromptu speeches and no expounding on his own ideas. I'm certain they would be contrary to ours, and we're just not going to take any chances. Are we on the same page, General Morrison? Can I tell my team that you have it all covered?"

"You can tell them exactly that, sir. I'll see myself out."

"Good day, General."

The tall, elderly man stood and walked over to his window, turning his back to the general as he walked away. He brushed a hand through his thick, manicured gray hair and then crossed his arms as he stared out the window and looked out at the skyline of the nation's capital.

* * *

Andre's funeral was a somber event. It was incredibly difficult for Donald. As he took the podium and delivered an elegant eulogy, he could barely force himself to deliver uplifting words to the gathered crowd of family and friends while knowing he was concealing the reality of what had actually happened to Andre. He was keenly aware of the high level of surveillance he was under. Every entrance to the hall where the funeral was being held was tightly controlled by Secret Service agents. They were also monitoring the outside lawn and parking areas. The agents were all so similar in their attire and bearing, they might as well be wearing uniforms. He had made countless campaign remarks about his predecessor in the White House constantly using a teleprompter. It upset him to now be under such control from others. The eulogy, as ordered up by General Morrison, was in front of him on the teleprompter. He was expected to read it verbatim. There was more than one person in attendance that noticed he had adopted this new practice of using a teleprompter after ridiculing its use so much. After the service, Donald remained silent and in deep thought on the drive back to the White House. Melania could easily read the concern in his expression.

"Are you all right, Donald? You've been withdrawn for the last several days, not just at Andre's memorial. Has his death upset you that deeply?"

Her words seemed to startle Donald, and he turned toward her. "I'm sorry, darling. Did you say something?"

"I asked if you were this upset over Andre's death? I mean, you haven't been yourself for several days. Would you like to talk with me about it?"

"I'm fine. Yes, Andre's death really hit me hard. It just reminded me of how fragile life is. He was fine one minute and gone the next. He was my best friend and a confidant. I'll miss his wise counsel. I was counting on him to help me through my obligations here. He was brilliant. He really was."

"Just know that I'm always here for you. Please don't shut me out. If you're concerned about things, it will be better for both of us to talk about it. Don't you agree?"

Donald reached over and gently placed a hand on her cheek as he looked deeply into her expressive eyes.

"Yes, absolutely. Andre's gone but thank God you're still here with me. I need you more than ever, Melania. You have to understand though that there will be things I cannot share with anyone, not even you. And there're going to be things that would probably upset you if we talked about them. I'll try to be judicious with the problems I bring home. Please don't think for a moment that anyone else has my ear more than you do. You've always been the person I trust the most. I'd never do anything to jeopardize that."

Donald lightly kissed her on the lips as the limousine continued ferrying them back to the White House. As soon as the kiss ended, Donald resumed his preoccupied stare out the window away from Melania. She stared straight ahead, but the concern was evident on her face.

✳ ✳ ✳

After two weeks in office, Donald was growing paranoid as to who was watching him and what monitoring devices were following his every movement. The agents and the cameras that monitored the nation's most important people and buildings were now more like guards in a prison to Donald, though the public perceived them as protecting the President. Cameras were positioned virtually everywhere. Donald received messages daily either from a courier or a phone call, telling him that he had gotten too loose with his words or thoughts and to be more careful with what he said and did. His every move was under surveillance, as were those of his family and staff. There was never a minute during the day when his mind was not going over any possible method of circumventing the system that was in place to keep him in line with the powerful forces now overseeing his every action. Just two days earlier, General Morrison had called him back to The Situation Room for a brief meeting. There were the same two young officers with Morrison as well as the Secret Service agents posted at the door. It was apparent the general trusted a few of his subordinates more than others. He directed Donald to once again take a seat.

"I won't keep you long Mr. President. You recently sent a text message to an old business associate named Stacy Mercer."

Donald immediately took a defensive posture, "It was strictly business. He is one of the managers of my blind trust. You know I can't manage my business interests while holding office. It's the law. I..."

"I do understand that, Donald, but there was one line in your text that I take exception to. Bring that up on the screen, Lieutenant Drexler, if you will."

The young officer turned on the monitor and used the remote to bring up a screen shot of the actual text that Donald had sent to his associate.

"That's good. Now, Donald. I believe it's the third line down. Yes, there it is, where you say, 'Stacy, we need to talk about a few developments here if you can break away for a day or so.' That's no good. First off, no one is invited here unless it's cleared through my office at least a week in advance. We don't mind you having company or old friends visiting you at the White House, but it's going to be a monitored and scripted event. No one comes if I don't personally call you and tell you it's approved. Got it, Mr. President?"

General Morrison's pronunciation of "Mr. President" had taken on an audible degree of contempt. It was becoming a slur.

Donald looked in disbelief at the monitor as he realized that they were able to intercept texts immediately from his personal smart phone that, to his knowledge, had never been out of his possession.

"I was not implying anything in regards to 'our relationship' here. It was going to be a business meeting. That's it."

"If you say so, then I believe it. I'm not here to call you a liar. I'm just telling you that impromptu meetings and texts with dialogue like this one, speaking of some sort of 'developments here' are not going to happen again without serious repercussions."

"Such as murdering another member of my staff?"

"That was not murder. That was suicide. Your Chief of Staff killed himself when he threatened our team. We had no choice. The fact is, that example will save lives in the long run. I'm sure you won't allow anyone else to put themselves in a position that we find threatening. I'm sure you see that."

"OK, General. I get your point. Anything else on your mind?"

"It's not in your best interest to take that tone with me, Donald. You and I both have the same objective, world peace. You are a mouthpiece for it, and I represent enforcement. Our goals are one and the same. And yes, there is one more thing. I don't want to see you perceived as some sort of shut-in at the White House. I have several trips in mind that I think would be good for you to make. For example, next week you will give a speech to our fine young cadets at West Point. That's where the leaders of tomorrow will be trained. I certainly want to do everything possible to encourage them. I'll have a speech prepared for you and sent over to your office sometime tomorrow. Look it over. If there's anything you think would improve its impact, you can make notations on it and send it back to me. I'll make a decision on your suggestions and get the final draft ready for delivery. I'll have my staff make all the travel arrangements including security for you. Feel free to take the First Lady and any of your family you think would enjoy seeing the campus there. It is impressive. You can leave now. Just remember what I've told you."

Donald turned without responding and walked toward the door. As usual, a Secret Service agent had it open before he got there. By now, Donald was refraining from making any gestures of appreciation to Morrison's minions. He understood fully who their real commander was, and it wasn't he.

✱ ✱ ✱

The Presidential helicopter hovered for a moment to lower its nose into the wind. After the aircraft stabilized, it slowly settled onto the parade grounds at West Point. A large gathering of cadets in rigid formation waited at parade rest. Just as Donald and Melania appeared in the doorway of the helicopter, the West Point band began playing a crisp rendition of Hail to the Chief. A smaller entourage of the university's commanding officers waited just beyond the range of the chopper's propellers to greet the President. As the engines were idled and propellers came to a halt, the group approached the President and First Lady. Donald extended his hand to the Superintendent in charge of the United States Military Academy.

"You must be General Prather. I've heard some very good things about you and how well the Academy is doing under your guidance. Good job."

"Thank you, sir. It's an honor to have you here with us. General Morrison requested a suite here on campus for you and the First Lady. Once you review the cadets here, we'll get you right over to your accommodations. Dinner at the mess hall will follow shortly thereafter. I understand you want to see how our cadets live and even where they eat while they're here."

"It seems like General Morrison is very much on top of things."

"Yes, sir. He's an extremely detail-oriented commander and it's an honor to serve with him. We've worked together on a number of outposts around the world and in at least two combat zones. Vietnam was where we really forged our strongest bond. A great man."

"I'm glad you're familiar with each other. It will make my stay here much more, predictable."

Donald understood the inferences that General Prather was making: the Academy was just as highly monitored as the White House. There would be no 'down time' from being under Morrison's watchful eyes. He and Melania walked over to where the eager young cadets were waiting to exhibit some of their drills to the Commander-in-Chief. Donald couldn't help but wonder if any of these young men and women had any idea what was going on with the military in the nation's capital. Their fresh, idealistic smiles gave him the impression that they had nothing but the highest degree of honesty and integrity. Perhaps he could find an ally of some sort among these young people. He couldn't afford to take any chances with the lives of his family and staff, but there had to be someone who was not in on the treason within the military complex. He would have to exercise extreme subtlety in his attempt to find someone within the ranks of the Academy. Perhaps no candidate would emerge, but he would be looking at them all closely. The drills continued for about twenty minutes. The strong winds and cold temperatures didn't dampen the overt enthusiasm of the cadets. It was an impressive display of synchronized precision. Donald wished he could take the palpable patriotism and meticulous work ethic imbedded in these cadets back to Washington and clean out the snake's den it had become. After the drills, General Prather directed two young cadets to escort the President and Melania to their quarters, along with two Secret Service agents who would also be staying in the guest quarters adjacent to theirs. As they headed down the brick sidewalk, the agents politely reminded Donald that their luggage would be following them shortly. It was refreshing to be in the presence of some young men who didn't have a three-day beard or have their bodies covered in the tattoos that were currently in vogue among so many young people. To him, those things represented the shallowness and superficial nature of a younger generation he didn't understand. It just looked dirty to him. These cadets carried a confident posture. Their deep-seated sense of responsibility and commitment to their fellow cadets, God and country was unquestioned. Donald moved up just behind them and engaged them in small talk.

"So, where are you men from?"

The taller of the two cadets responded in a strong Southern drawl.

"I'm from Georgia, sir. Columbus. Near Fort Benning."

"Yes, I'm quite familiar with that area. Beautiful old Southern architecture."

"Yes, sir. That's just one of the things I love most about it. My family has lived there for several generations."

"What's your name, young man?"

"I'm Cadet James Grimshaw, sir. I'm very pleased to meet you."

"It's a privilege for me as well."

Donald looked toward the other cadet. "And your name, son?"

"Robert Melville, sir."

"Like Herman Melville?"

"The same, sir. My father says we are distant cousins. You've read 'Moby Dick'?"

"Of course. Hasn't everyone?"

"I imagine so, sir. I'm from Seattle, sir."

"Very good. You are both a long way from home. How are you enjoying your studies here?"

Responding first, Cadet Grimshaw said, "If you don't like discipline or resent authority, this is not the place for you. It's strict. If you don't follow the rules, your time here will be very short and unpleasant. I don't have a problem with the rules. My father retired from the Army and so did my grandfather. Many of my ancestors fought for the Confederacy."

"Being from Georgia, that doesn't surprise me at all. So your dad was a soldier as well, huh?"

"That's right, sir. He was a Ranger in the Special Forces. He retired in the eighties. He did two tours in Vietnam and earned two Purple Hearts. He was a great inspiration for me to attend here. When I got my Congressional appointment, he was the happiest I'd ever seen him. I'll do good here and make him proud."

"That's very commendable, young man. You can't go wrong thinking that way."

Cadet Melville joined in with, "My dad was in the Navy. He kidded me quite a bit about going Army. Even as a young boy, I always wanted to come here and have a career in the Army. I don't care where they send me. Even if it's to the Middle East. I'll be graduating this spring and I hope to become a platoon leader somewhere that there's action. I don't like pushing papers or marking time."

"Very commendable, but be careful what you wish for. The Middle East is a powder keg that seems to have no possibility of a peaceful conclusion. No matter where you're sent, you'll do fine, Melville. I'm sure your father will be proud as well. For that matter, America is proud of you."

Donald knew if they understood fully what was going on at the top, they would be out of there by dark. However, they were so young and he doubted they could grasp the magnitude and depth of the conspiracy. One word to the wrong person and people could die. He would weigh his course very carefully during the visit.

The next morning, Donald and Melania woke to the magnified sounds of reveille over the parade grounds' loudspeaker. It was unmistakable. Thousands of young troops were falling out onto the grounds en masse and at a dead run. Within seconds, they were in tight formation. Loud commands that needed no amplification to be heard were being barked to the cadets. The young men and women responded in unison. In short order, most were headed to the mess hall. West Point was not just a military academy; it was a world-class university that offered a top-notch education for a commitment of time and life to the nation. Its many illustrious graduates included military heroes and Presidents. Donald and Melania got dressed quickly and alerted their Secret Service guards and a cadet outside their door they were ready to head out for breakfast at the mess hall. After the meal, Donald would deliver his address to the students and faculty at Eisenhower Hall Theatre. As they walked through the campus, they were impressed by the classical grey stone buildings encircled by incredibly lush countryside. West Point was built on the banks of the Hudson River, about fifty miles north of New York City. It was impressive in every regard. Donald hoped he might find an ally in the midst of this epicenter of idealism and nationalism. After a full breakfast with the cadets and officers at the mess hall, Donald and Melania were led to the Eisenhower Hall Theatre. They entered the stage from a back entrance. After his introduction, Donald moved to center stage. As he approached the podium, the cadets and officers came to their feet at attention. Donald could clearly see the teleprompter that was set up just in front of him and to his right. Until Andre's funeral, he had never before used one. He resented it being there. Still, there was too much at stake to circumvent it at this point. He would use the teleprompter speech, but he would make his opening statement on his own. General Morrison and his team could stew about it all they wanted. It was a small pushback, but he would do it so they would understand that his will had not been broken. Donald smiled as he addressed the eager cadets.

"At ease. What an absolute delight this is to be here with you this morning. As you can see, the First Lady is here with me as well."

Melania smiled at the audience and then sat in a padded chair alongside the commanding general and several other dignitaries in attendance.

"We were both impressed with your drills last evening and with this magnificent campus. This is my first visit here, and I can honestly say that any American would be proud to see this Academy and you fine cadets. I'm also struck by the dedication of all you fine young men and women who will soon take your places with others in the ranks of our military, and undertake the tremendously important task of guarding our country. You are to be commended for your hard work and dedication to the United States. One thing I want you to think about is the commitment you make when you take the oath to defend your country against all enemies, foreign and domestic. That's the promise to lay your life on the line for your country. No one makes a more serious promise during their lives than that. Don't take it unless you intend to live by it. Over the next few months, I hope to visit some of the locations throughout the world where our military has a presence. I want to personally thank them for their service and let them know that our citizens understand they are there protecting freedom."

From that point on, Donald read the speech prepared for him on the teleprompter. It was basic and offered no insights into where the United States was headed or what any of its leaders were undertaking. It disgusted him to have to deliver such an ordinary speech to an extraordinary group of patriots, but this was not the time or place to exercise an open rebellion. The cadets gave him a rousing applause at the conclusion of his speech. He felt unworthy yet waved appreciatively to them. After helping Melania up from her chair, he escorted her off the stage. He noticed that cadet Grimshaw, whom he had met the previous evening, was waiting back stage.

"That was an excellent speech, sir. I'm very fortunate to have been here to hear it. I will remember your words as I go to my duty assignments."

"Thank you, James. I would like to have said a little more but time constraints and national security always come into play."

"I understand, sir. Nonetheless, it was impressive."

"Is there a restroom nearby? The First Lady might need one as well."

Melania smiled.

"Yes, sir. I'll be glad to show you where they are. If you would, follow me just down the hall, sir. I'll take you there."

"Excellent."

Aware that Donald was stepping out of the prescribed path that was laid out for him, the Secret Service escorts contacted each other immediately using their lapel mic radios and alerted one another as to this small change in plans. Cadet Grimshaw directed them to adjacent doors at the end of the hall. Always leery of any deviation, one of the guards entered first, scanned the small room, then indicated to Donald that it was clear to enter.

"Mr. President, I'll be just outside the door here if you need anything."

"I'm sure you will. I'll only be a moment."

Donald knew his time would be short. He entered the stall inside the room that contained the toilet. He withdrew a pen from his jacket pocket and a business card from his wallet. On the back of the card he quickly printed.

"Presidency under siege by the Joint Chiefs. A silent coup. Trust no one here. No media or government, any level. Need outside help ASAP. Call the White House and say you're Francis Marion. I'll be expecting your call. I'll lead the conversation. D. Trump."

Donald flushed the toilet, went to the sink and let the water run for a second as if washing his hands. He took the card and kept it palmed in his hand. He needed to somehow get it to the cadet without raising any suspicion from his guards who were always just a whisper away. He stood outside the men's room and waited until Melania emerged shortly afterwards. He turned toward Cadet Grimshaw.

"Lead on, James."

"Yes, sir."

"By the way, James."

"Yes, sir?"

"You mentioned your father and what an inspiration he is to you. You indicated he served several tours in Vietnam, isn't that right?"

"That's correct, sir."

"There's a service held each year at the Vietnam Memorial. I wonder if he'd like to be my guest while I give a speech and lay a wreath there."

"I'm sure he would be absolutely thrilled to attend, sir. I doubt he'd even believe you spoke to me about it. How would he get in touch with you about coming?"

"I'll give you a number for him to call and we'll make all the arrangements."

Donald turned to the lead Secret Service agent.

"Thompson, do you have a piece of paper or a card I can write a phone number on for this young man?"

"I think I have a card with me sir, but that's all."

"That would be perfect. Do you know the White House phone number?"

"Yes, sir. It's the main switchboard number. Is that OK?"

"Just what I wanted. Can you write that on the card as well for this young man?"

"Yes, sir."

The agent got out his wallet and found one of his cards. After writing the phone number on it, he handed it to the President not thinking for a moment there was anything going on other than a gesture toward a cadet. Donald then handed it over to the cadet. He slid his handwritten card underneath the other one. He figured that would draw no suspicion as the agent assumed the cadet was only getting his own card with the phone number he'd written on it.

"Now son, make sure you get this to your father as quickly as possible. I'd love for him to come to Washington for the ceremony."

"Yes, sir. He'll be honored. I'll mail it out right away."

"That's great, son. Now, let's get on back to the chopper before they leave without me."

"I'm sure that wouldn't happen, sir."

"I hope not."

Donald and Melania boarded the helicopter, which already had its rotors spinning. They waved to the cadets as the door closed behind them. Within moments, it was out of sight headed back to the capital. James was awestruck about the time and attention he had personally received from the President. He reached in his pocket and pulled out the card he had been given. He was startled to find the second card in with the other one. He held it closer to his eyes and read the message scribbled on it. Confused at first, he read it twice more before he grasped the gravity of what he held in his hand. He excused himself from the other cadet and double-timed it back to his dormitory room. He found his cell phone buried beneath the socks in his dresser. At first, he was going to call his father that minute from his room, but then thought it might be safer to go out on the athletic field and find a quiet corner to make the call.

"Son, how are you doing? Is it cold up there?"

"Not so bad, Dad. I can't talk but just a minute. I think this is very important. Let me read something to you, so I can tear up the note."

"What are you talking about?"

"Please just listen, Dad. I told you I was one of several cadets chosen to escort the President and First Lady around campus during their visit here last night and today."

"Yes, I am incredibly proud of your being chosen."

"Well, something really bizarre happened."

"What's that?"

"President Trump slipped me a note to give to you."

"You're kidding! What on Earth for? I'm sure he doesn't know me from Adam."

"He asked me about my parents. When I told him you were a retired Army Special Forces Ranger, he asked me more about you. As he was leaving, he had a Secret Service agent write the number for the White House on one of his cards. The agent handed it to Mr. Trump who added his own card to the agents. On his, he asked me to give you this number and have you call him right away about attending a Vietnam Memorial wreath-laying ceremony. The note said you were to use the name Francis Marion when you called and let him do the talking."

"That sounds very strange."

"Wait till you hear the rest. Here, I'll just read you the note. 'Presidency under siege by the Joint Chiefs. A silent coup. Trust no one here. No media or government, any level. Need outside help ASAP. Call the White House and say you're Francis Marion. I'll be expecting your call. I'll lead the conversation. D. Trump.' What do you make of this?"

"Son, if that's all true, then the country has a huge problem. Listen, you don't tell anyone about the card he gave you. I'll do what he asked, but you tear up that note in very tiny pieces immediately and get rid of it. You never saw it. If anyone asks you about it, play dumb. Did anyone see him give it to you?"

"He asked a Secret Service agent to give me his own card and write the number at the White House on it. The agent gave that card to the President who must have slid this other card under it when he handed it to me. I don't think the agent suspected anything."

"Don't take any chances. Keep the card the agent gave you in case anything comes of this, but get rid of the other one now before you do anything else and make sure nobody sees you doing it. The pieces need to be so small and scattered nobody could ever put the note back together. And, son..."

"Yeah, Dad."

"Remain calm no matter what happens. Always deny knowing anything about this. I'll take it from here on out. Do you understand completely?"

"Yes, sir."

"OK. I'm on this. You go back about your normal routine. Don't worry if you don't hear anything about this from me. I must operate under the highest degree of secrecy with my people and figure out who can and can't be trusted. Talk to you soon, son."

"OK, Pop. I love you."

"And I love you, son. Your grandmother isn't here right now but I'm sure she would tell you she loved you too. Bye."

"Bye."

James hung up the phone and began tearing the note up in pieces smaller than a penny. Thinking more about it, he tore them all in half again. He took the pieces and dumped them in tiny groups into different trash receptacles from the athletic field all the way back to his room. Just as he dropped his phone back into the dresser, his roommate, Cadet Dennis Morris, entered and startled him.

"Boy, are you jumpy. What's up?"

"Nothing. Just put the President and First Lady back on their helicopter. I'm stoked to say the least. I'm heading over to the mess hall to get some chow. You interested?"

"I just finished before I came back here. I can go with you if you want me to. You can tell me how things went with the President."

"OK, that sounds good."

The two young men left to go have dinner. James kept the unusual events of the day to himself as his father had asked him. Though he was committed to doing his part, he was still anxious about where all this was headed and even more concerned with his father's involvement.

* * *

Alone late at night in his ornate penthouse office, the clandestine leader of the group leaned back in his tufted leather chair, put both hands behind his head and stared upward as he spoke over the speakerphone.

"So, Morrison, you felt the visit to West Point went well from our viewpoint?"

"Yes, sir. Nothing unexpected. Trump and his wife were in close proximity to one or more of our people the entire time. Even when he used the latrine, our people were right at the door listening to make sure that taking a piss was all he did."

"Good, good. We appreciate your thoroughness, General. That's why you are where you are. So he seems to be conducting himself as we have directed him. And he engaged in no private conversations with anyone?"

"Absolutely. Our people were literally standing alongside him from the moment he landed. The only people he even spoke with were a couple of young cadets as they escorted him to the parade grounds and to his suite. No one to worry about."

"We worry about everyone, General. And I never underestimate what an idealistic young man is capable of doing. You of all people should appreciate that fact. If it weren't for teenagers, it would be almost impossible to have a war or an army for that matter. If my memory serves me well, a number of West

Point cadets withdrew from school to fight in the Civil War, isn't that correct?"

"Absolutely! They served brilliantly on both sides. When that war broke out, many cadets dropped out of school to go back to their home states and fight."

"My point exactly, General. These cadets Trump spoke with. Anything at length or regarding, how shall I say it, touchy subjects?"

"No, sir. He did deviate on his opening remarks for his speech, adding a line about what cadets need to consider when taking their service oath. I'll speak with him about that when he gets back. I'm sure it was just to let us know he still has a mind of his own. Kind of a stupid thing to do but he's sort of strong minded that way. He'll learn. Then, after his speech, he gave one young cadet a card with the White House phone number on it so his father, who is a Vietnam vet, could come to the Memorial and help him place the wreath."

"Really, a card, huh? And where did this card come from? He just happened to have one in his pocket at the ready for such an occurrence?"

"No, sir. I already asked that question. He didn't have anything with him to write on, so he asked one our agents for a card. The agent used his own card, wrote the number on it for Trump and the President handed it to the kid."

"I see. So, general, here's what I want you to do. Immediately have one our people find this cadet. I don't care what time of day or night. Retrieve that card for me. That was a break in our rules and no matter how simple it may seem. I don't put anything past Trump. Don't underestimate him. He's a brilliant man. If you think he's not continuously plotting on how to get rid of us, then you're not quite as smart as you may think you are. It may be totally innocent, as you say, but I didn't get where I am by taking anything for granted. Get that card and call me. You understand?"

The general was agitated at the inference that he might have overlooked something that was so obviously of no consequence, but he nonetheless complied with his superior.

"Yes, sir. Tonight."

"That's all."

To add emphasis to his displeasure with Morrison, the leader hung up without further comment.

✳ ✳ ✳

It had been a long day for James Grimshaw at the Academy. The excitement of a visit by the President and the honor of escorting him around the campus were overshadowed by the startling message and personal request for help he had received from the President. His mind hadn't stopped racing since that time. He felt no immediate threat from anyone, but he was smart enough to understand that if all that the President had indicated was happening were true, then he would have been monitored throughout the visit. He did have agents and guards around him constantly. If this was a military coup, then there would have to be someone at the Academy who would have insight into it. He would have to be extremely careful from this point forward. As the President and his father directed him, he would trust no one and discuss nothing of this incident with anyone. It was hard to fall asleep with all of this rattling around in his head. He was exhausted, yet full of adrenalin. He lay face up in bed, aware of nothing other than his own concerns and the heavy breathing of his roommate. He wanted to sleep, but couldn't seem to fall over the edge of consciousness. Tomorrow would be difficult without rest. There were no light days for a senior at West Point. He finally closed his eyes and started to drift off. Seconds later, an alarming burst of lights and the unmistakable sound of boots on the floor of his room shook him back to consciousness.

"Cadet Grimshaw."

"Yes, sir. I'm Cadet Grimshaw. What is this all about, sir?"

"I'll be asking the questions. Get out of your bed."

Grimshaw recognized two of the Academy's staff officers and was dumbfounded to see General Prather standing behind them. At first, his confusion over the purpose of all this overpowered his sleep-deprived brain. Then as his mind switched into high gear, he knew with ever-increasing clarity what this visit must be based on the events of earlier that day.

"Good evening, Cadet Grimshaw. Do you know who I am?"

"Of course, sir. You are General Prather, Superintendent of the Academy."

"Good. I need for you to answer a couple of questions for me."

The general looked over at the roommate.

"Cadet, what's your name?"

"Morris, sir. Dennis Morris, sir."

"Slip your pants on and walk down the hall 'til we call for you, Morris."

"Sir, yes, sir."

Completely alarmed, Morris threw on his pants and literally bounded from the room. Questions to superiors regarding orders were never tolerated. As he left the room, one of the younger staff officers closed the door behind him and the general stepped forward.

"I understand you got to spend quite a bit of time with President Trump today. That correct?"

"Yes, sir. It was a huge honor."

"I know, son. I agree completely. I've met several sitting presidents during my career and it's always a very exciting experience. I'm glad that you appreciated the moment. My question for you is this. The President gave you a card, a business card with a phone number on it. Is that correct?"

"Yes, sir. He did."

"I'm told by a member of the President's security staff that the agent who gave you the card and wrote the number for you apparently gave you the incorrect number. He gave you a confidential and top secret number that is reserved for the Secret Service to alert the President in case, God forbid, there was ever an attack or serious threat against the White House. That agent had to memorize that number and is only supposed to give it to people with top secret clearance. You understand what I'm talking about?"

"Completely, sir."

"And do you still have this card with the number on it?"

"I do, sir. I was going to send it to my father so that he could set up a visit to the Vietnam Memorial when the President lays a wreath there."

"What an honor. I'm sure your father would be thrilled to receive that invitation. However, the number you were given is not the one he should be calling. We'll get you the correct one tomorrow. Now, I'd like to retrieve that card from you if you would be so kind."

"Of course, sir. It's right here in my dresser."

The instructions Grimshaw's father had given him were turning out to be of grave importance much sooner than anyone could have imagined. Fortunately, at this point, the only card left in his possession was the one given to him by the agent. James opened the dresser drawer. Before he could reach inside, one of the officers pulled him back and the other removed the drawer and dumped its entire contents on the cadet's bed. Grimshaw was shocked by this aggressive move. He remained silent and watched as the officer rummaged through the exposed contents. There was only one card in the drawer.

"Here it is, sir. It has just the one number on it like he said."

"Let me see it."

General Prather looked it over closely on both sides. Confident it was just as Grimshaw had described, he turned to the cadet.

"It's fortunate you had not sent this to your father yet. You can see how important security around the President is. It has to be that way. The world is a very dangerous place. That's why you and all the other cadets here are being groomed to handle these problems in the future. Now, I'm ordering you to remain totally silent about all of this matter, the card, the secret phone number, anything you were told about it by President Trump. And don't discuss any of this with your family either. You certainly don't want to involve them in a security issue, do you?"

"No, sir. I understand, sir."

"You're a good cadet and will make a fine officer. I'll be keeping an eye on how you do after you graduate. It always makes me proud to see how far our young men and women can go. I think you will go quite far, Cadet Grimshaw. Good night."

"Good night, sir."

The trio of officers left the room as quickly as they had entered. Dennis Morris came back into the room as soon as they were clear.

"What on earth was that all about?"

"Nothing, Dennis. At least, nothing I can talk about. Let's try and get some sleep. Five a.m. will be here quickly and I need sleep."

Neither cadet would sleep for the rest of the night.

✹ ✹ ✹

General Prather made the late night call to General Morrison.

"I have the card in my possession. What do you want me to do with it?"

"Send it to me via courier, labeled Top Secret. Do you know if the cadet had given any information to his father yet?"

"He said he was going to send the card to him. The card had only the main number for the White House on it. Crisis averted. Nothing to worry about, really."

"We worry about everything. And he indicated to you he had made no calls yet about the card?"

"He didn't say."

"Well, we'll be checking on phone records immediately just to be sure. Like you said, it all seems innocent enough, but we must verify everything. Thanks for the late night help."

"My privilege, General Morrison."

"Good night."

General Morrison was in his office before the sun came up. Younger staff officers were constantly coming in and out handling a myriad of details. The general didn't like to see anyone who wasn't fully engaged and busy. They all knew it. He motioned to Lieutenant Drexler.

"Come over here a minute."

"Yes, sir."

"There's a young cadet at West Point named James R. Grimshaw."

"The one who received the card from the President yesterday?"

"The same. I want you to find out who his parents are, where they live and what they're up to. I want all of Cadet Grimshaw's phone calls tracked since yesterday morning. I also want his future calls monitored until further notice. See if he called his parents' house at all yesterday."

"Do you have his phone number?"

"Oh yes, it's right here in my pocket!" The general said with sarcasm and a pause. "No! I don't know his number, but every kid in America has one of those smart phones that lives in their ear. Find his number and track those calls. Got it?"

"Yes, sir. Sorry, sir."

"Just get on it."

✷ ✷ ✷

Major James M. Grimshaw, U.S. Army Retired, lived alone in a small home in Columbus, Georgia. The place could use a woman's touch. Nothing was where it should be. He stayed clean and always freshly shaved. When clothes needed washing, they would just hit the floor of the small laundry room and remain there until either the mood struck him to do the wash or the path to the washer was nearly impassable. His friends called him Jim. His wife, Audrey, was a native of Columbus. She had passed away from cancer five years earlier and left him a young sixty-five year old with two boys to finish raising. His firstborn, Robert, had graduated from college and was teaching high school in Arkansas. His younger son, James, set out to follow in his footsteps with a career in the military. Being an Infantry Officer Candidate School graduate who got his college through night school, he'd insisted his son go to West Point if he could get in. He felt that being a West Point officer was a better course to follow than his own career path. Both tours in Vietnam had ended with a Purple Heart and one with a Silver Star. Discipline, responsibility and honor were traits he put high on his list of what a good soldier must possess. He pulled every string and called everyone he knew reminding them of any favor he'd ever done for them to get his son the congressional appointment it took to be accepted and admitted to West Point. To have James there preparing to graduate with honors, gave him a sense of pride and fulfillment unequaled in his life. He just wished Audrey could have lived to see it. He was particularly troubled by the call from James, whom he called Jimmy. His mind had been racing that morning trying to come up with some sort of plan. His time in the military gave him a keen insight into just how deep and thorough a military coup would have to be to attain the degree of control it apparently had now reached. The corruption would have to start at a high level and run very deep. By necessity, the tentacles would run throughout every agency and department. It would be next to impossible to trust anyone in the capital when formulating a strategy. It was just as well with him though, as he had been building his own list of trusted friends with the skills and experience it would require to undertake such a dangerous counter scheme against high ranking military leaders. He knew their mindset well. He'd worked with them, for them and in spite of them for many years. To his mind, the biggest problem he would face would be overcoming the government's high degree of technical monitoring. No phone call, text, letter or face-to-face meeting could be considered safe from surveillance. As he stood by the coffeemaker in the outdated kitchen, he was deep in thought. Help from trustworthy allies would be the only way he could move forward. The phone next to him on the counter rang. He was on guard from hello.

"Good morning, Jim. How are you this morning?"

"I'm OK, Mom. The question is how are you feeling?"

"Oh, I'm as good as any eighty-eight-year-old can expect to be. Hey, I need a little help from you right away if you can."

"OK. What's up?"

"The toilet is backed up and I can't flush it at all. I shut off that valve under it with the knob that you turn. That cut off the water, but now it won't flush and it's stinking up the whole house. Can you run over here for just a minute and look at it? I won't keep you, I promise."

"I'll be there in five minutes, but I can't stay. Got a lot of stuff going on over here today. Friends coming into town and all. I'll tell you about it later."

"OK, dear. See you soon."

"Bye, Mom."

The last thing Jim needed to do was go to his mother's house to fix a stopped-up toilet. He figured it would be easier to just go handle it than to delay it by giving her an excuse about why he couldn't come right away and answer questions about what he was up to. He figured that in ten minutes, he could get it unplugged and get back to what had to be the most important task in his lifetime. He quickly made his way over to his mother's house.

"Hey, Mom. Which toilet is it?"

"The one next to the laundry room. Come on, I'll show you."

Mildred Grimshaw, known as Millie to her friends, took Jim by the hand and led him toward her laundry room. As they entered, she closed the door behind them and hit the start button on the washer and dryer which were apparently both ready to be utilized. Jim was confused by her actions.

"Forget to cut them on earlier?"

"There's nothing in them. Come over close, I've got to whisper this to you."

Now Jim was over-the-top curious.

"What on earth are you up to, Mom?"

"Jimmy called me really early this morning. He said your phone calls coming in and going out are going to be monitored. Some general came into his room last night and picked up a card. He said you'd know what he was talking about. Do you?"

"Yes, go on."

"He said not to worry, it was not the card with the message on it he read to you; he did what you told him with that one. He said he told them nothing, but said that you need to be very careful in any communications with anybody, not just from phones but anywhere there could be a camera or somebody listening. He called me because he said they would be listening to your calls, not mine. He called on a friend's phone from school. Now, can you tell me what this is all about? If I didn't know what a serious young man Jimmy is, I'd think this was some sort of prank. But it's not a prank, is it?"

"No, Ma'am. Look, the less you know about any of this, the safer you will be. Don't talk to anybody you don't know or even with your friends about this. Nobody! If Jimmy calls you again, you can just call me and tell me the toilet is overflowed again. Yeah, that will work. Other than that, forget it happened. Please."

"OK, Jim. But this reminds me a lot of how you were back twenty-five years ago. Coming and going without notice, all times of day and night. Never knew if I'd ever see you again. And Audrey, bless her heart, was worried sick about you all the time. She'd be so proud to see them boys of hers now. I miss her so much."

"Me too, Mom. But look. I've got to run right now. Remember, you know nothing and we never spoke about this."

"Of course, Jim. You be careful."

"I will. Don't you worry."

"Yeah, right."

6

It was late in the evening in Washington, D.C. All of the posh watering holes were still going strong. Government and corporate credit cards were burning up card readers all over the capital. By day, millions of government workers who were toiling away at middle management, secretarial and blue-collar jobs tried to fill their day by at least looking busy. Most understood that in the larger scope of things, they were mostly non-existent to those who ran the show. The people who actually called the shots, made the decisions, and doled out billions of taxpayer dollars were holding their meetings in rooms with polished mahogany bars, crystal chandeliers and grand pianos. The two-hundred-dollar bottles of wine were being uncorked faster than the black-shirted wait staff could run to the coolers and return them to the tables. The movers and shakers were lubricating the wheels of commerce with the oil furnished by hundreds of millions of hardworking, unimportant citizens. A few of the people in the upper echelon were not in their usual haunts this evening. Their limos were pulling up in front of the gleaming tower where all the serious decisions were actually being made. Normally the inquisitive eyes of the media would see their movements, but tonight they were unloading their occupants with no media presence. They had been given strict orders that no cameras or reporters would be working in that area that night. These were not only the heads of every government agency controlled by the conspirators; there were powerbrokers from most major industries and the media gathering for the conclave. Seated at the front of the room were the men and women who ran both political parties. Their faces and names were known by almost everyone as they had been continuously on radio and television in the last election cycle giving every ounce of concentration they had to try to stop the public from electing Donald Trump. They understood clearly that this meeting would formalize a position regarding how to handle this uncontrollable maverick in the White House. They had all seen this night coming, but had not yet found a way to stop it. Their leader stood behind a small podium at the front of the room.

"Good evening to you all. I appreciate your being here. I'm sure you all suspect the reason this meeting was called. Donald Trump is a major problem to our organization, as we knew he would be. I've heard from the board today and spoken with most of them personally. They are concerned. We have too much time and money invested here to watch this buffoon destroy it all. Our primary financial backers wanted me to get you all together tonight and let you know what we're planning. You understand, the brothers and other board members have invested billions in the infrastructure and take very seriously any problem that might disrupt the normal business operations they control on a global level. They are interested in your thoughts, opinions and any suggestions you might have. Let's start with the media. Jack, what are you seeing regarding the public's perception of the President and the government?"

The well-known network president stood and turned to face the group as he spoke. "The public clearly thinks something is wrong. They just don't know what it is. Because they don't understand how everything really works, they just think that government is broken. Their personal income is down relative to the rising costs of living. Obviously, taxes have gone up considerably to cover the cost of what has to be done to meet our goals. The byproduct of that has slowed business growth in the blue-collar sector. Small business costs have gone up with the new taxes, especially with our new national healthcare program. The money just isn't there for employers to pay low-end workers more, so they're falling behind. Frankly, they're pissed. We all know what our goals are tonight and we're all on the same page. However, I don't see how we can hold the entire country hostage without the public getting more and more angry."

"Ah, you underestimate us, Jack. I agree we've overreached a bit and at a little faster pace than we should have. And some of the things we thought might help the global situation backfired on us. Most notably, the 'Apology Tour' by the President was not a good strategy. Granted, it emboldened a lot of the small players around the globe and ignited some conflicts that produced a strong bottom line for our group over the past eight years. But, as you indicated, it caused a lot of anger here at home. It was smart to wait until most of the World War II veterans were dead and Vietnam era personnel were too old to put up much of a fight against us. Yes, they're unhappy with where the nation is headed but what can they do about it now? They're just too old. That was brilliant. The current generation of young voters is the result of twenty-five years of permeating our group's priorities throughout the national school system. That has worked out just as we had hoped it would.

Today's students and even university graduates are absolutely clueless about their own history and they don't give a damn as long as they can live in their low-information, virtual world. They are the perfect citizenry to mindlessly go about their business as we run ours. How about some input from the political front? What do you party activists think of what's going on with 'The Donald'?" He held up his fingers to illustrate a quote as he spoke the name. His face curled up with ridicule at the same time.

A well-known spokesman for the Republican Party took his turn speaking to the group. "We did everything we could to stop him. We tried to stack the delegate count to make it almost impossible for him to win, but the voter turnout was so huge that we couldn't overcome the numbers. We tried to force it into a contested convention. Then it became obvious that if we offered anymore pushback against the voters, they would probably riot at the convention. It would have been a complete disaster and brought too much unwanted attention to our process. So, he got in. I don't know how many of you are aware of the amount of money we spent trying to keep him out, but it was well over a billion dollars. In several states, we spent over a hundred million each. That's huge in an election."

Their leader interrupted, "To put that into perspective, a hundred million or even a billion is not that much. A single fighter jet now costs over a hundred million. Orders have been coming in all year, especially from the Middle East for the latest and greatest weapons on the market. Things are in turmoil right now. But I am certain when I explain to you what we are going to do, you will agree with us. It's apparent that Donald Trump will not work out for us as President. However, his Vice President, whom we handpicked, is with us. He becomes President and this all becomes just a dark and brief page in our country's history. The media will love the amount of attention, and advertising dollars, this will reap."

Another television network president stood up. "Are you saying we have to kill Trump?"

"No, not at all. We aren't going to do anything so brutal here in the States. The public would never stand for that. He's getting ready to take a trip into a very volatile section of the world. Yemen, to be precise. Right now, there's a civil conflict going on over there. It's a dangerous place. Very dangerous. Anybody flying over there would be taking their life in their hands. I think you can see where this all ends."

The network president, with a startled look on his face stood back up. "I, for one, am not happy about this. I didn't sign on to commit murder, especially to assassinate the President."

"Brent, no one did. However, I will remind you that you have personally benefited from being aligned with us. You were nowhere near the front of the line to become president of one of the country's premiere networks. I'm sure you'll agree with me there. And now, we are where we are. You'll be in far worse shape if this doesn't happen than if it does. I urge you to think carefully about what you say and do at this critical moment. We are counting of each of you here tonight to do your part. In two weeks, this will be just a footnote on the pages of history, and we can all get back to taking care of business. I think we've about covered all we needed to this evening. I will remind you all that secrecy is not only expected but required of you. No exceptions. I'll be in touch with most of you personally over the next few days. Any announcements on the news must be approved by this office before it goes live in any fashion. Now, have a good evening. We will contact you with any updates about these events in Yemen."

7

Donald sat at the end of the very long conference table in The Situation Room alongside his new Chief of Staff, Sidney Aldridge, the well-connected New York attorney who had replaced Andre Whittal. Donald could barely stand to be in the room, as he knew anything discussed there would be completely controlled by General Morrison and his minions. He could still see Andre lying on the floor struggling for his last breath. To him, this room was no longer the nucleus for top-secret meetings and high-level decisions; it was a crime scene. And the crimes continued unabated. General Morrison sat in his usual place at the head of the table. Standing behind him once again was Lieutenant Drexler and several other subordinates.

"Mr. President, the reason we're here is to update you on an ongoing military situation which is escalating in Yemen. Are you familiar with the factions that are at war there?"

"Yes. I have a close friend from my college years whose family owns hotels throughout the Middle East. Even though they're based in Dubai, they have quite a few properties in Yemen. I've been there before to visit him and his wife. He introduced me to President Hadi, and I've been in contact with him many times over the last several years. I understand there is a military faction there trying to oust him. They are well-armed and growing in numbers. They seem to be well financed. Many people believe we are furnishing the rebels with high-tech weaponry, but I'm certain that we would never do anything as unethical as that. Right, General?"

The question was asked with lots of insincerity to let Morrison know that he didn't trust anything he might say.

"Of course we're not aiding the rebels to overthrow the legally elected government of any nation. I think my being here to express our concern over the situation should allay any fears you may have on that issue. We think you should visit Yemen and express our support for President Hadi. Perhaps by visiting with him and making a public show of support, it might discourage the rebels from continuing to attack the larger cities. Of course, we want to make our latest weapons available for purchase to President Hadi as well. With your support and more powerful weapons, it should sway the tide of military actions toward the government and emphasize our position to the Yemini leaders that the United States is an ally that can be counted on. We'd like you to visit with him next week. We already have security staff en route there to establish the highest degree of security while you're there. Would you want the First Lady to accompany you and perhaps other staff such as Mr. Aldridge here?"

"I definitely don't want to leave Melania here while I'm away. It would be very interesting to know exactly who films her dressing every morning and getting ready for bed in the White House every night. Of course, there are probably websites where you can hire perverts to do just about anything. That's where you came from, isn't it, General? To answer your question, Mr. Aldridge can stay behind and manage the office. Crime in the nation's capital seems to be getting out of hand lately. You can't feel safe anywhere, not even in the White House."

"I appreciate your quick wit, but you're certainly overstating the case, Mr. President. I can assure you that it would be impossible for any harm to come to you or the First Lady while you are under the protection of the Secret Service and Capitol Police. There are dedicated people looking out for you every moment of every day."

"You certainly said a mouthful there, General. And when does Air Force One leave for Yemen?"

"Sunday evening. You'll be in country and ready for meetings the next day. All the necessary arrangements have been made. We'll have a statement ready for Mr. Aldridge here within the hour so he can release it to the press. All of the news agencies are interested in covering the developments there and have requested their reporters be allowed to ride with you on Air Force One. I'll give you a list of acceptable names and you can pick the ones you'd like to be on the plane with you. Nothing worse than spending time with someone you don't see eye to eye with, is there?"

"Your clichés are right on target today."

"Don't forget, Mr. President, you can talk things over with Aldridge here as I'm sure he's aware of our arrangement. But other than you two, no one else has the clearance to discuss with you anything that our group brings your way. Total silence by you in these confidential matters is required. It's for your own safety, and that of your families. You both understand?"

"We understand completely, General. Completely."

"Yes, well, good evening then."

Donald and Aldridge left the room before any of the military staff. The less time Donald had to look at them, the better. He knew they had dramatically underestimated him. He'd bide his time and play the part of the fool for now, but a reckoning was in the making. There were days ahead that General Morrison and his team could not see. Retribution would be swift and severe. Donald would see to it personally. As they walked down the hall and back toward the Oval Office, they talked quietly knowing full well they were being overheard every moment.

"Mr. President, you were not exaggerating a bit. I had no idea it had gone this far."

Donald turned to look directly at his new Chief of Staff.

"No one would believe this. Its sheer magnitude makes the concept difficult for anyone to believe. If I didn't know what I know now, I'd have problems seeing it as even being possible."

As he looked at Aldridge, he said with a slight smile, "Their control is so complete and thorough that no one could even begin to think of a way to overcome them. You can see yourself that it would be impossible, I'm sure."

Realizing that Donald was using sarcasm to make his point without saying anything that could be overheard and misinterpreted as hostile, Aldridge responded, "Yes, sir. You are correct. Their control seems to be total. It would be stupid to try to subvert them. I agree completely."

Points made, the two men continued on to the Oval Office.

✳ ✳ ✳

General Morrison's staff car pulled into the parking garage located in the basement of the tower. Earlier in the week, he had arranged for Vice President Snowden and their leader to have a face-to-face meeting. Several younger officers and bodyguards from the Secret Service exited from a second vehicle immediately behind them. They scurried ahead to open the doors and secure the private elevator to the penthouse. They all stared blankly ahead as they made the journey to the top floor. Conversation between them was almost non-existent. The office they were heading toward was foremost on their minds. The door to the suite opened just as they approached. As they entered, their leader had his back to them as he was looking out the window of the gleaming tower.

"Come in, Vice President Snowden, General Morrison. Can I have some tea or coffee brought in for you? Either of you?"

"I'm fine, sir."

"And you, Mr. Snowden?"

"None for me either. I'm quite anxious to hear about what is going on. I'm aware of Trump's visit to Yemen. With all the turmoil over there right now, is that safe? I mean we don't want to see a newly elected President in danger, do we?"

After a prolonged pause, the reply was not what Snowden expected. "Yes, Mr. Vice President, I'm afraid we do. You see, President Trump is not working out the way we had hoped he might. He's a very strong-minded individual, and he has not taken very well to the arrangement between his office and ours. We're concerned he might make a risky and pointless attempt to usurp our authority over the office of the President. He's already made a stab or two at probing our security net around him and his family. It's just a matter of time until he does something really stupid. We can't afford to let that happen."

"How can you prevent it? If he just speaks out to the media or contacts someone else who might do it for him, how can you prevent that from happening?"

"You see our problem clearly, Mr. Vice President. We've dealt with issues like this before when a President thinks they control the bully pulpit. In the past, a few well-placed reminders of what could happen to them or their family and they would toe the line. Not so, I'm afraid with Donald Trump. So, we've gone ahead and made plans for you to become President. Tomorrow to be precise."

"Tomorrow? What are you talking about? Are you going to ruin him, catch him in some sort of treason or what?"

"None of that. His reputation will be intact. He will enter the annals of history tomorrow as an honorable servant of the people who met an untimely end at the hands of insurgents in the Middle East. There's already a revolt under way in Yemen where he and the First Lady are headed tomorrow. It will rise to a crescendo late in the evening and a lawless bunch of rebels will attack the Presidential palace. A most unfortunate event. You will be sworn in by sunrise the following morning. The nation cannot be without a President for very long. From here on out, we will not allow anyone to run for the office who is not one of us. It was never a good idea and I fought against it from the start. From here on out, we will own the presidency. So, you need to go get some rest. You will be extremely busy over the next week. When we call on you, do just as you're told. No questions. You work for us. Understand?"

"I do, sir."

"Good, now go get some rest. General Morrison, you need to stay here a bit longer as we have a few additional arrangements that need to be made regarding tomorrow's events. I don't want anything to happen by chance. You can call for another car when we're done."

"Yes, sir."

✷ ✷ ✷

Air Force One made a graceful and impressive landing at Sana'a International Airport in Yemen. Even as the large aircraft was taxiing over to a secure area, Donald could see through the windows that security was everywhere. It was not just airport security. There was a large presence of government troops. They were standing on the tarmac in formation. Military vehicles, including several tanks, were stationed a few hundred yards away. Coming in to land, he could see that all roads leading into and away from the terminal were being intensely patrolled. There were multiple checkpoints along the approaching roadways. It was apparent that things in and around Yemen were not normal. There was the ever-present threat of a rebel attack throughout the country. President Hadi was taking no chances with President Trump and the First Lady visiting. He needed to enlist their support quickly if he was going to be able to suppress the insurgent factions and save his country.

As the Trumps walked down the steps of Air Force One, he was the first in line to greet them. As Donald offered his hand, Hadi clasped it with both of his. A look of both stress and relief could clearly be seen on the leader's face. He understood that without help from the U.S., his country would soon be overthrown. Through a heavy accent, he greeted Donald and Melania in English, "What an honor to have you both here. To have you visit us now will be a large blessing to all of the loyal citizens of Yemen. Solidarity with the United States means so much to all of us here. Thank you for coming."

"It is our pleasure and duty to be here so that you can see the United States stands by its allies. The Middle East has seen more than its share of problems. You and the loyal people of Yemen have been a partner we have counted on through all of these times. It's wonderful to see you."

Standing directly behind President Hadi, Donald could see his old friend Azim. President Hadi noticed that he recognized him.

"And, Mr. President, as you can see we have invited your old and dear friend, Abdul Azim and his wife Uma to be here to welcome you."

Donald and Melania warmly greeted Azim and his wife.

"My great friend, Azim, it's wonderful to see you again. How long has it been?"

"Far too long. We need to catch up during your visit."

"I intend to do just that. I understand there will be a dinner this evening at the palace. Will you and Uma be there?"

"We wouldn't miss it. There is so much to talk about. There are many problems here. I know President Hadi intends to enlighten you with all that is currently happening. So we shall look forward to the evening."

"Good, we will see you then."

President Hadi spent a few more minutes introducing Donald and Melania to key members of his staff and the leaders of Yemen's army who were all in attendance. Shortly thereafter, they were whisked away to a suite on the palace grounds where security could be tightly controlled. It looked almost as if they were visiting a military base in Iraq during the Persian Gulf War with the presence of so much military. Donald assumed that must mean the rebels were in very close proximity to have this much heavy firepower at the Presidential Palace. After Donald and Melania quickly freshened up, there was only an hour before the State dinner would begin. Donald had been given a list of talking points by General Morrison, who assured him that his every word would be monitored. He was told to stick as closely as possible to the script. It was infuriating, but the general and his group held all the cards. At least they did for now.

The Presidential Palace in Yemen had a distinct Arabic architecture. The two large ivory-colored towers were highlighted by light brown stucco with clay-tiled roofs. Graceful in design, the structure could have been used in a production of *Arabian Nights*. However, being surrounded entirely by razor wire and guarded at every entrance by a heavy military presence did visually distract from the overall beauty of the large complex. Staff and guards were posted at all of the palace doors.

Current leaders of both the government and military, dressed in their finest formal attire and uniforms, filled the large entrance hall. Most spoke little or no English. Donald and Melania spoke no Arabic. An interpreter was present every step of the way to make certain that each greeting was properly conveyed to and from the Trumps. For most of those present, the American President represented the last hope for saving their country and perhaps even their lives. Azim and Uma stood patiently at the end of the line of government and military dignitaries. They were the first civilian guests to greet them. All the guests thanked them profusely for coming to Yemen.

President Hadi escorted them through large double doors into the State Dining Room. A small musical ensemble played smooth indigenous songs in one corner of the room as everyone took their seats and waited for their meal to be served. President Hadi stood and welcomed everyone to the affair before the serving of their multi-course dinner began. Donald felt certain that this was the first dinner of its kind to be served in the room for some time. Certainly, no parties or social events were taking place in a palace besieged by its enemies. Yemen was putting its best foot forward, desperately reaching out to Donald and his military for help. After dinner, there was a brief social gathering where guests could approach President Trump and the First Lady.

After an hour of socializing, President Hadi adjourned the festivities. He turned to Donald and Azim. "President Trump, I wonder if the First Lady might enjoy a tour of the palace while we talk about Yemen and our state affairs in my office."

Overhearing the offer, Melania responded, "I'd be delighted, President Hadi. I'm fascinated by your culture, the architecture and art. You and Donald take your time. I'll be pleasantly engaged."

President Hadi and a few key staff and military leaders led Donald and Azim to a secure conference room deep within the palace. The room was full of ornate fixtures, draperies and paintings. Donald took a seat at a highly-polished conference table, as his friend Azim sat alongside other officials and distinguished army officers. Donald had to insist that an accompanying Secret Service agent be allowed in the meeting as well. He thought to himself how shocked Hadi would be if he understood why the guard had to be present. After everyone was seated, Hadi jumped into an immediate plea.

"President Trump, I am certain you are aware of the critical moment in which we now find ourselves. Yemen will soon be ruled by Islamic terrorists if we do not receive help from the United States. The rebels have great financing from Iran, and several other two-faced countries we both consider allies. They speak constantly of peace and tolerance and then fund many madrasas where they preach hate and intolerance even to small children. You do remember that fifteen of the nineteen 9/11 conspirators were Saudi nationals? They take your oil money, pretend they are your allies, and then fund terrorists. That is what we are dealing with. Even the countries the United States saved during the great World Wars have no problem selling warplanes, missiles and guns to terrorists. We do not even know whom we can trust. We need your help. We are near the end of our resources. Our citizens cannot get to work so there are no taxes with which to fund our efforts with armed insurgents running all over the country killing anyone they find offensive. Soon we will not even be able to feed our soldiers. No one is coming to our aid. Can we count on the United States, and on you, for support? We could turn this all around very quickly with your country's assistance. These rebels have no stomach for a fair fight. They go into a village, behead the elders and any young men who make any attempt to resist. The women are raped or taken to serve as prostitutes. They have even killed small children. They are savages. If we had strong help, we would have them on the run in ninety days. I know this is so. Will you help us?"

Donald knew he could offer nothing without the backing of the military and thus General Morrison. He couldn't express to President Hadi the incredible irony that the United States had already been taken over by rebels. He could only say he would bring it up to his government and present the case for support.

"The United States isn't run by one man, not even the President. I can tell you I am very sympathetic to your plight. I will make every attempt to enlist the support of the U.S. Congress and the Pentagon. To be honest, I can promise nothing other than my most earnest effort to solicit support for Yemen. That you can count on, President Hadi. I'll get on it as soon as I return to the U.S."

Abdul Azim joined in with a plea of his own. "Donald, we've known each other a long time. We've had a number of business relations. You are an honest and forthright person. I trust what you say. Even though I'm not a resident here, I have many businesses – hotels, commercial enterprises and business associates here. President Hadi has my full support. He has the best interests of his people at the forefront of his concerns. Before the rebels began this assault on Yemen, the country was beginning to prosper. Business was good. Many investors from all over the world were coming to help build up the economy. All of that has been destroyed in the past six months. There is nowhere in all of Yemen that is safe anymore. When we landed here today, we were fired upon by machine guns just outside of the city. My pilot says we took several rounds through our tail section. No one will risk coming here anymore under this scenario, and we do not blame them. I will continue to do all that I can for my friends here. They asked me to speak to you on their behalf. That is why I am here asking you to intervene, to help bring a stop to this madness."

"Azim, I am certainly on your side. I have no stomach for these insurgent animals that are bringing terror everywhere in the Middle East. The only thing they understand is force. They cannot be reasoned with. Back in my country, many do not understand that these are people who want to kill others more than they want to live. I understand they must be stopped by a modern and powerful military force. You have my word that I will go back to my country early tomorrow and bring whatever influence I can to get help for the people of Yemen. As I said before, I can't promise anything but I'll do what I can. After I speak with those who are in a position to make the decision, I will call and let you both know the outcome. My plan is to get this done this week."

President Hadi looked directly at Donald as he spoke, "I can only say, do all you can as we may not have a week."

"I promise, I'll do all I can. You have my word on that."

"Well, I know we are all very tired. President Trump, I'll have you escorted back to your suite. The First Lady is already there."

"Thank you. Please believe me when I tell you that I am on your side."

"I do."

Abdul Azim put his arm over Donald's shoulder.

"Come, my friend. I'll walk with you back to your room, and we can reminisce about better times."

"I would enjoy that, Azim."

The vigilant Secret Service escort walked just behind them within earshot of their every word. Donald was glad to see his old friend. He wished they could spend some time together in a more congenial environment without General Morrison's ears walking alongside them. He wondered if he would ever be free of his monitors.

"How long will you be here, Azim?"

"I'll be leaving in the morning. Your plane should be leaving about the same time, so we'll probably see each other at the airport. To tell you the truth, I'm a little nervous about flying out of here. After taking a few rounds in my plane on the way in, it's obvious that there are rebels in very close proximity to the airfield and probably close to where we are right now. I'm certain they know you are here. Nothing would please them more than to be able to capture or even kill the American President."

"I feel like we have pretty good protection. The Secret Service has been here for over a week to make sure we're safe during this trip. They're good at this stuff. You have a security team with you, don't you?"

"When you're in international business, like I am, you better have security with you all the time. Even at home, there's always the threat of kidnapping or some other nefarious scheme underway. You just can't be too careful."

"You're right. It's a constant concern. The world seems to be getting more dangerous all the time. Well, here's our suite. Thanks for walking with me. It's been good seeing you again. In case we don't run into each other at the airport, give our best to Uma and you take care and be safe."

"You too, Donald."

Inexplicably, Azim reached out and gave Donald a brief hug. "If we don't meet again, it was good to see you, my friend. Good night."

"Good night to you as well, old friend."

The Secret Service agent held the door open for Donald to enter.

"The room is clear, Mr. President. The First Lady is already there."

"Thanks."

Donald was blunt but polite to the agent. He wanted the least amount of familiarity with any of them as possible. He walked over to the bed where Melania was reading a magazine. She dropped it as he approached.

"It seems like they are having a lot of problems here right now. The woman in charge of housekeeping told me there have been killings, kidnappings and routine firing of weapons right here within the city limits over the past couple of weeks. What's the issue?"

"There are rebels trying to overthrow Hadi. He wants us to support him and place some troops and weapons here. I really don't know if that's possible."

"Isn't it your decision as Commander-in-Chief to put troops on the ground?"

Donald wished he could answer, but he was certain every word they said was being overheard by Morrison's agents, so he said, "I'm not certain what comes under my discretion at this point. It's one of my highest priorities when we get home. I'm exhausted. I know you must be as well. Let's turn in and call it a day."

"I love you, Donald. You know that, don't you?"

Donald leaned over and kissed his wife on the cheek. "I do. If I ever forget to tell you, remember that I do and I always will. You are the reason I get up every morning and the reason I'm glad that I'm still here at the end of every day."

"You are a sweet man, Mr. President."

"And you are a lovely First Lady. Good night, darling."

"Good night."

✳ ✳ ✳

The first rocket slammed into the palace around two in the morning. The impact was severe as it struck. Donald and Melania not only heard the explosion, but felt the ground quake. They watched as the glasses on their nightstand fell to the floor. Melania looked over at a dazed and confused Donald. "What was that?"

"I have a feeling the palace is under siege."

Within seconds, small arms fire could be heard from all corners of the compound. Donald eased over to a window and looked out from one small corner.

"Don't turn on any lights. We don't want anybody seeing our shadows in here."

There were tracer bullets and flares lighting up the square. Sirens started to go off within the palace compound. Donald jumped up and started to dress quickly.

"Get dressed, Melania. We've got to get out of here now if it's still possible to leave."

There was heavy pounding at the door. Donald asked through the door who was there. The Secret Service agent assigned to watch their door replied, "It's Williams. The compound is under attack. You and the First Lady need to come with us to the airport ASAP! They're bringing the car around now. Just get some clothes on and leave everything else behind. We have to go now!"

The urgency in his voice was real and Donald knew it. Melania was remarkably calm as she grabbed some clothes to put on.

"Donald, do you think we'll be all right driving to the airport? I mean, it's several miles. Who knows what and who is waiting? If they know we're here and that Air Force One is our way out, surely they're counting on us to make a run for it."

"We just need to listen to the Secret Service and do what they say. Most of those guys have been in combat before. Remember, they don't want to die either. Are you ready?"

"Let's go."

Donald and Melania rushed out the door where three agents were now gathered. They were carrying M16 carbines along with their handguns and were wearing bulletproof vests. They had two extra vests waiting.

"Here, Mr. President. You and the First Lady need to let us put these on you. I'm sorry, but it's for your protection."

"No problem, we want them."

By this time, the sounds of rifle fire, grenade launchers and automatic weapons were constant. The sky was lighting up every few seconds with some type of ordnance exploding on the grounds.

Williams spoke to one of the other agents, "Harris, it's only going to be a couple more minutes and they'll have the range on this place. We need to be out of here before mortar shells start landing. What's the best way out?"

At the same instant, the group was joined by a half dozen heavily-armed soldiers assigned to guard the palace and President Hadi. The highest-ranking officer spoke to Donald and agent Williams. I'm Colonel Rashid. President Hadi has just been evacuated. We are to take you to the airport. There is a tracked, armored vehicle at the back entrance to the palace. We'll take you there and get you on board. The helicopter has already been hit. It's no longer an option. Follow us."

The Palace guards took the lead. Donald and Melania followed them. The Secret Service agents clustered close behind the group. Donald was concerned about what type of forces awaited them outside the Palace walls. The entire compound was shaking from the impact of multiple explosions. The lights went out for five seconds and a motor could be heard starting. The lights flashed on and off momentarily and then came back on much dimmer. Rashid spoke in short bursts to the group.

"The generators cut on automatically. Power to the compound has been cut. I can hear our vehicle running just outside. I'll lead to make sure it's safe. Williams, you and your men get the President and First Lady immediately to the door as soon as you see it open."

The Colonel opened the door and started to run the twenty feet to the waiting vehicle. Tracer bullets could be seen going in every direction of the compound. As he ran out, he immediately started to draw fire. Halfway to the vehicle, he took a shot directly in the chest. Even though his vest stopped the penetration of the shot, the impact knocked him to the ground. One of the junior officers directly behind him stopped and bent over. He threw his shoulder under the Colonel's and dragged him to the armored car. As he pushed him into the vehicle, the young officer took a direct shot to the back of his neck. His head banged into the side of the vehicle so loud it shook Donald and Melania several yards behind him. Melania let out a short scream.

Donald, shaken by the sudden death of this courageous young man, yelled to Melania, "Just keep moving. There's nothing anyone can do for him. He's gone. Hold my hand, and run as fast as you can. Whatever you do, don't fall down."

They gave every ounce of strength they had to the run for the waiting vehicle. The noises were deafening. The unmistakable sound of bullets bouncing off the armored car and impacting the pavement all around them set their adrenalin on fire. Pieces of pavement, broken loose from the striking bullets, struck them as they ran. Several men behind them groaned as they were hit by the live fire. Neither turned to look back. It would be a miracle if any of them escaped under such a heavy barrage. When the last man got into the vehicle, it was apparent that neither the Secret Service agents nor the young officer who tried to rescue the Colonel had survived. The Colonel was lying on the floor of the half-track still trying to catch his breath. Between gasps, he asked those who made it, "Is that everyone? How many are lost?"

Another Yemen soldier responded, "Three were hit. All are dead. Two were Americans plus Aran. He was the one who helped you aboard."

"I will remember him and glorify his name forever. We must go now."

He yelled from the cargo area to the driver, "To the airfield as quickly as possible. Don't stop for anyone, not even a roadblock. Keep your speed up. We have this one chance only."

The vehicle lurched forward. It was large and heavy with four huge tires forward and the rear sitting on large revolving tank tracks. The sidewalls were heavy steel impenetrable by any small arms fire. The rebels had already shown they possessed rocket-propelled grenades capable of doing serious damage to a vehicle of this nature. Luck would play a huge part in making it to the airport.

Donald asked the Colonel, "Is Air Force One operable? Is it ready to fly? Surely the rebels know it's there."

"I spoke with the airfield commander fifteen minutes ago. The insurgents were approaching the field with a small convoy of trucks and troops. Our men were setting up a perimeter wall as far around the strip as possible with the men they have. Some areas will be exposed because there just are not enough men to guard it all. We'll need Allah's help to make good your escape."

Melania grabbed Donald's shoulder and slid over tightly against him. Tears were streaming down her face. She was trying to be as strong as possible, but she was terrified of what lay ahead for them. The prospects for survival in this coup were dwindling by the second. The sound of bullets bouncing off the sides of the halftrack was relentless. Occasionally a flash of light would go off on the side of the road with a simultaneous sound blast that caused their ears to ring for several seconds afterwards. The vehicle would even lean away from the blast as if struck by gale force winds. As the driver looked out through the bulletproof front window, he could see the shadowy outline of the airport tower with every explosion that went off behind it. Immediately ahead, he spotted small trucks with machine guns mounted in their beds parked across the roadway. Over a dozen menacing figures holding rifles surrounded the vehicles. He realized these rebels were going to try to stop the tracked vehicle barreling toward them at all costs. Handheld spotlight beams were directed at the windshield into the eyes of the driver. The Colonel could see what was happening as well.

He directed the driver, "We cannot stop under any circumstances. A fifty caliber won't penetrate our steel. Increase your speed and go directly at the vehicles. Don't stop, I tell you. Mr. President, hold on to your wife and brace yourself. There is going to be an impact."

The large diesel engine powering the vehicle screamed louder than the explosions going off in virtually every direction. Dense smoke covered the road between them and the roadblock. Bullets were still smashing into the side of the vehicle. It seemed nearly impossible that they would actually make it to the 747 waiting for them at the airfield, and even less of a chance that the aircraft would still be in one piece. It felt as if their armored vehicle would come apart from the sheer strain of how fast it was being driven.

Seeing that the wall of vehicles was only yards away, the driver yelled, "We are going to hit them right now!"

The force of the crash knocked everyone forward against the two front seats. Their speed was slowed but for only a second. The driver floored the gas pedal and continued on. The sound of bullets moved to the back of the vehicle. The thought that a rocket launcher might soon be taking aim at them was on everyone's mind. It would have been of some momentary relief had they known that rebel commanders had directed the launchers to be brought to the runway so they could take aim at Air Force One if it started to move. The rebels' main goal was to capture the giant aircraft. They could gain immeasurable publicity worldwide with a video of the President and First Lady being forcibly removed from the airplane. They could be ransomed for a fortune.

Donald asked the Colonel, "How much farther to the airport?"

"It's just ahead. They have all the lights turned off, even on your plane. Don't want to light up a target. They know we are on the way and they are expecting us. Driver, do you see the shadow of the tail of the plane ahead?"

"Yes, sir. What do you want me to do?"

"The main door has a set of steps leading up to it. We need to pull up alongside them, as close as possible. Turn so that the back of the truck can be opened onto the steps."

"Yes, sir."

As they pulled onto the tarmac, the firefight escalated. The rebels must have guessed who was in the halftrack. The vehicle came to a stop and the shelling all around it intensified.

Colonel Rashid spoke hurriedly of his plan, "Mr. President. My two men will jump out first. You and the First Lady should go with them. I will follow with my driver. We get only one chance at this."

As they exited the vehicle, they could hear the engines starting on the 747. The entire area was pitch dark except for the rapid explosions. They could see fire shooting out from the jet's engines. The door was opened on the back of the armored vehicle and the two Yemeni guards exited. After stepping out, the second guard turned his back and offered a hand to Melania.

Donald yelled at her, "Jump, Melania. Go as fast as you can. Run up the steps. She dropped one leg from the truck and took the guard's hand. At that second, a burst of heavy machine gun fire from the end of the runway cut him almost in half. He fell dead to the ground in front of her. Melania screamed and pulled herself back into the truck. They were taking heavy ground fire from every direction. Rashid pulled the door closed. The second of the Yemeni guards almost made it to the plane. With multiple hits from rifle fire, he was killed ten feet from the metal staircase leading up to the plane.

Colonel Rashid gave commands to the driver, "We can't make it to the plane. We need to clear out from here and try to escape to a safe house. I know a place we can go until our troops can secure this area. Some additional troops will be here soon. Head to the other side of the main hangar, Asan."

The driver floored the vehicle. He turned in a short a circle and headed away from Air Force One as it started taxiing down the runway. The boarding ladder had not been pushed away, and the large tail fin of the plane knocked it down as it passed. They were not going to go to the far end of the five thousand foot runway and turn around. They were accelerating the jet's engines as hard as they could in an attempt to take off using only half of the usual distance. The less time on the ground, the better. The insurgents saw the jet starting to head off the airstrip and directed all of their firepower toward it. The halftrack containing Donald and Melania sped off in the opposite direction. They could hear the engines of Air Force One screaming as it hurdled toward the far end of the runway. It was making an all-out effort to clear the ground before the end of the airstrip. It began to lift its nose off the ground just as their halftrack turned behind the hangar. The landing gear on the front of the plane clipped the fifteen-foot barrier fence at the end of the runway. In an effort to reduce all drag possible, the pilot retracted the landing gear within seconds after the fence fell over. The hangar that the halftrack was aiming for was located in the middle section of the main runway. It was equidistant to either end of the airfield. Donald looked out through the small rear window of the halftrack trying to see if Air Force One was clear of the airport. They were not far off the ground when he saw the trail of a surface-to-air missile heading directly upward from the end of the runway. Donald watched in horror. It was a direct hit. The explosion rocked the entire airport area and everywhere within five miles of the horrific crash that ensued.

Donald gasped as he spoke, "She's down. They hit her. Air Force One has been destroyed. A missile hit it just after it cleared the runway. It's in a million pieces. There's a fireball on the ground. All those people. Many, many good friends."

Melania and the Colonel could see the red glow reflected on the glass pane Donald was looking through.

Colonel Rashid spoke up, "The other aircraft that brought your support staff here is already gone. They must have made it out before the insurgents got too close to the airport. Perhaps some of your friends were on that one."

"That would have been mostly Secret Service or military personnel. Looks like they would have stayed behind to help the others."

"I'm certain the rebels will assume you were both on Air Force One. They must think you were killed on that plane. Surely, it wouldn't leave without you. This may buy us a little time."

At the back of the hangar, Asan noticed two men waving a flashlight. He slowed a little to see if he recognized the men.

Colonel Rashid looked toward them as well. He knew one of them immediately.

He turned to Donald. "One is your friend from Dubai. Should we stop and try to pick them up?"

"Yes. We cannot leave him. Pull over quickly."

The Colonel directed Asan to turn toward them and stop as close as possible. For the moment, the hangar had the halftrack obscured from the main rebel force but he knew that would only be a temporary situation. They opened the rear door.

"Azim, it's me, Donald. Get in quickly."

"No, they will find you and it will be over. I have a better idea. My jet is in the hangar. It's very fast and has room for all of us. We can take off in the opposite direction. Uma and my staff are already aboard. We must hurry though. There are many rebels in the area. They are overrunning everything. Come with me now."

Donald thought of his options and could see no other course that had any chance of success. He turned to Rashid. "Colonel. Let's go with Azim."

"I cannot, Mr. President. My country needs me here at this moment. I'll get clear from here and we'll regroup tomorrow or the next day. We have to take back our country. I must stay and fight. You and the First Lady should go with Mr. Azim. That's your best chance. May Allah be with you!"

Donald reached out and shook the Colonel's hand firmly. "We owe you our lives. We'll always remember what you did here tonight. Godspeed."

Donald and Melania dropped out of the halftrack and raced back inside the hangar with Azim. The jet was already running with its nose pointed out of the open door on the backside of the hangar. The aircraft's door was open and there was a small set of steps leading up to the cabin of the private jet. Azim literally pushed them quickly up the stairs. A waiting guard from Azim's private security force shut the door behind them. They each grabbed a seat.

Azim directed the pilot. "Alright, let's try and make good our escape. Give it everything we have."

The pilot pushed the control lever giving the gleaming white jet full throttle even though there was a left and right turn to reach the main airstrip from the hangar. The plane accelerated dramatically, lurched forward and leaned over ten degrees with each of the turns. By the time it reached the main runway, it was already doing over forty knots. As it straightened out its course, the acceleration became dramatic. It would require a much shorter distance to be airborne. The pilot spoke in Arabic over the internal speaker.

Azim translated for Donald and Melania, "He says there are vehicles coming from behind us as fast as they can. Nevertheless, he says, 'They are trucks and we are a jet so they will never catch up to us.' Once we're airborne and out of range of their shoulder rockets, we're safe. They have a few helicopters but no jets. We're flying with no lights and very low to stay off their radar."

Looking out a small window to the battlefield they had just left, Donald could see a large fire on the ground where Air Force One had crashed. It was lighting up the night sky for miles. Melania leaned against him and sobbed into his shoulder. This horrendous night was unlike anything she had ever been exposed to in her privileged life. It was a reality check about how much of the world lived and died. Their lives had taken a very dark turn. Donald would fight back to lift his country out of the cesspool it had become. In the midst of all this misery and despair, one fact suddenly crossed his mind: There were no longer any Secret Service agents or United States government officials with them, monitoring his every word and movement. There was his old friend, Azim, his wife, Uma, , a couple of his aides, the pilots, and two personal security guards plus Melania. In all, there were ten people on the plane.

Donald turned across the narrow aisle to Azim. "Where are we headed?"

"Ultimately, Dubai. Right now, my pilots will have to get permission to cross air space. Remember, we are a jet aircraft leaving a country in the midst of a war. Other countries will be on guard for any aircraft that is not theirs attempting to fly over their territory. You cannot blame them."

"I understand."

"Should we try to make contact with officials back in the United States? They also will think you were on Air Force One."

"No. Absolutely no contact for the moment. There is a lot going on in the United States that will shock you, old friend. You and I need to have an in-depth conversation about what my next steps should be. What we just experienced back in Yemen has already occurred back home. Very few shots were fired, and my people don't even realize there has been a revolution."

"What are you talking about, Donald?"

"You'll find out shortly. Until then, please no contact with the U.S. at all."

"That's how it will be. I'll tell my staff and pilots this is all highly confidential."

Landing in Dubai was almost like being back home. The busy international terminal was lighted to the point only an experienced pilot would have any clue which runway was the correct choice.

Skyscrapers filled the background. Thousands of car headlights streamed throughout the city streets. Though at times, too much congestion in a large city had gotten on Donald's nerves, tonight all of these urban signals brought comfort. The jet set down peacefully in Dubai and at last they were safe, at least for the moment. With his vast influence within his own country, Azim's jet regularly left and returned without having to go through the formality of a customs inspection. In this instance that would prove to be invaluable.

✱ ✱ ✱

Azim was a wealthy man, just like Donald. In their respective worlds, both held a great deal of power and influence, controlling vast financial empires. His offices occupied the entire top floor of a modern skyscraper in the heart of the commercial section of Abu Dhabi, a modern city of over two million people. Azim and Donald sat alone in his palatial office. Floor-to-ceiling windows on two sides offered a spectacular view of the metropolitan area located on the south shore of the Persian Gulf. In recent years, it had become a major center for commerce in the United Arab Emirates and a showplace for the Arab world. To be a big player here meant you were also a force in the world economy. Donald had known Azim for many years and trusted him as much as he trusted Andre Whittal. He felt confident discussing with him what he had been going through back in the States.

After listening to Donald for over an hour, Azim appeared dumbfounded. "This is truly unbelievable, Donald. If it were anyone other than you telling me this horrific saga, I would think they were either insane or lying. But here you are, and I know what you say is real. What must be done to bring an end to this travesty? To restore America to a true democracy? The remainder of the world must not know of this. It would cause untold turmoil, emboldening our mutual enemies, and placing the entire world in danger. How is it possible to deal with this?"

"I'm thinking it over as we speak. I can't make any rash moves. They control a large section of the major news outlets and local governments from Washington, D.C. down to individual states and even cities. It makes it very hard to know whom to trust. If the wrong people get a hint of any sort of threat to their power, they will come after us with everything they have. Trust me, that's more than any other country could deal with. I have to be very careful."

Azim pointed to a large television mounted on an interior wall. "Have you seen what is on the American news channels this morning?"

"Not yet. Melania was still asleep and I didn't want to wake her. She was exhausted and traumatized by what she went through yesterday. I want her to sleep as much as possible so I came straight here. Turn it on and let's see how General Morrison and his band of terrorists are spinning this."

The set was already on CNN. They were showing aerial video footage of the fiery wreck of Air Force One. The bottom of the screen was flashing with a summarizing statement.

"The President and the First Lady killed in vicious nighttime raid in Yemen."

An announcer was describing the events.

"We are awakening this morning to the horrific news that President Trump and First Lady Melania Trump were both aboard Air Force as it made a desperate late night attempt to take off from the airport in Sana'a, the capital city of Yemen. Reports are still coming in. The support plane that routinely accompanies Air Force One on trips to foreign countries did make it out just ahead of the shelling that resulted in the downing of the President's plane. Those aboard the first plane saw the explosion just behind them and said there was absolutely no way anyone could have survived the crash. Let's go now to the Capitol where Vice President William Snowden will be sworn in as President later by Chief Justice John Roberts. Ron Archer is there live. Ron, can you tell us where things stand right now?"

"Yes, Martin. In spite of all that has to be going on here behind the scenes, I can report that the normal protocol is being followed so that there is a seamless succession of power from the late President Trump to the Vice President, soon to be President, William Snowden. I understand there's been an outpouring of condolences from the leaders of foreign countries, both allies and adversaries. A makeshift memorial has been building all day alongside the fence at the White House. Though a very short-lived presidency, Donald Trump and his wife Melania were widely loved and respected. His message and avowed purpose to bring a change of direction in this country from a very strong and centralized government back to a more state-centric government was very well received by the average American. It has been a tragic presidency as well. Everyone remembers that within hours of his inauguration, an accident took the life of White House Chief of Staff Andre Whittal, and now this. I'm told the swearing-in proceedings will take place very soon, so I'll turn it back over to you, Martin. I'll be here to cover the ceremony when it begins."

"Thank you for that report, Ron. We'll be checking back in with you periodically throughout the morning as you follow the events unfolding there. A very sad day, indeed."

Donald was turning red in the face as he listened.

"That's enough, Azim. Turn it off please. Snowden is a snake. I was forced to pick him up as a running mate to secure votes in some key states. At least that's what I was made to believe. Now, the real reason is so damn. They not only can tell the President what they want out of him, but they own him. I must devise a way to bring all of this out into the open. The biggest problem is that they control the military. Any hint of even a small revolt would be met with overwhelming military action. These are incredibly dangerous people. They control the entire power structure of the strongest nation on the planet. Trust me, if they had even the most remote idea I was here with you, there would be some catastrophe taking out this entire city block instantly. They'd tell the world press what happened: 'A previously undetected fault in the Earth's crust under this building caused a massive earthquake' or 'another coup by the military' occurred right here. Yes, they're extremely experienced with coups. It's their specialty when it comes to dealing with smaller foreign nations. In the U.S., it barely causes a raised eyebrow when we hear that another despot or would-be Napoleon has overthrown the government of some country. There has to be a way to circumvent their control, to get the public to realize what's been done and get them to turn against the group directing this mayhem. I have to come up with an invincible plan. Any thoughts, Azim?"

"Most countries in the Middle East have lived under the threat of revolution for generations. Our people grow up expecting war and unrest. We are nations made up of City States, almost like small feudal kingdoms. Leaders come and leaders go. There is always bloodshed and destruction. Then there is peace for a while until it starts again. However, there is one rule that dictates all of these despots, as you call them."

"What rule is that?"

"In the United States, it's the old saying 'cut off the head of the snake and the rest will die.' You find out who is running the entire thing and eliminate them. You will not have to face the military at all if they are without their leader. Kill the king you might say."

"I agree, but in this instance, I don't even know who the king is. It's so clandestine that the only person I've had any dealings with is their front man, General Morrison. He runs the entire military through the Joint Chiefs of Staff."

"Then that's where you must start. If you grab the tail of the snake, it will turn its head to bite you. Am I right?"

"There's no doubt that Morrison knows who is behind this whole scheme. If we could get him alone without a large circle of protection, I think we could make him talk. To save the country, I'd be willing to start with waterboarding and go from there. He's evil and wouldn't understand anything less than that. You know, I was one of the only candidates running for President who was decisively in favor of waterboarding by the military. Most of the politicians were against it or lukewarm to the idea, saying it was inhumane and that I was a monster for being willing to use it. Now, here I am seeing waterboarding as the minimum of what I'd be willing to authorize to save my country and its people. All it takes is a dose of reality to change a person's point of view."

"I think it's obvious that military action against those running the U.S. is not possible. It would be short and brutal. With what we now know, I'm sure there would be no survivors, no one to tell the truth. So how can you get to this General Morrison?"

"First, we need to speak with some of the people I trust. I have not been able to have a private word with anyone since I took office. Hell, they probably even have a camera in my toothbrush.

Melania and the kids were monitored. Literally, they watched every breath we took. They sent me the day's agenda every morning and made it clear that any deviation from their messaging would be met with severe retribution. They weren't above going after my wife, my kids, and even my friends. I need to build a coalition of people I trust absolutely. If any one of them broke the trust, we'd all be dead. I'll work on those key people today. I need to get back to Melania. She's bound to be up by now and I want to be there for her. She's going be very upset."

"I understand. You want to meet again after lunch?"

"Yes. I'll think through all this and try to have some sort of approach figured out by then. Thank you for not only saving our lives, but for all your support as well. You've been a great friend and ally for so many years."

"That's what friends do, Donald. I'll see you later today."

Donald hurried back to the suite that Azim had so graciously provided for him and Melania. For a change, there was no Secret Service agent assigned to his door. Azim had a central security force that guarded the entrances to the building, monitored the halls and general offices with cameras. There was still privacy in individual meeting rooms and suites. Donald entered their suite and saw that Melania was up and dressed. Her clothes were the same as they were wearing when they fled the palace. Other than the clothes on their backs, they had left with nothing. In spite of that, Donald felt relief that for the first time in several days, they could talk privately with each other.

"Donald, are you OK? I was concerned. Once I realized you were gone, I couldn't go back to sleep. So many people we knew died yesterday. It's heart-breaking."

"I know, darling. I've been thinking of their families all day today. Have you eaten anything yet this morning?"

"I haven't even thought of food, but I would like some clean clothes to change into. Do you think that's possible?"

"I'll ask Azim. This is a big city. We can send out for some. We can't take any chances of either of us being seen here. We'd be in a great deal of danger if they thought we made it out alive. They are counting on us being dead. They've probably already sworn in that weasel Snowden by now. We would be a real threat to their plans. And we are going to be just that."

"What are you talking about? Who are these people you're talking about and why would they want us dead?"

"I haven't been able to explain this to you because I've been under their continuous surveillance up until now. It's a relief to be able to tell you without fear of anyone listening. Sit down and prepare to be in disbelief over what I'm about to tell you."

Donald spent the next hour describing in great detail what had happened all around him since he became President. Melania was stunned.

"What about our kids? They think we're dead too. How can we get word to them without anyone else knowing?"

"That's exactly what I'm thinking about now. I need to come up with a couple of folks that I can trust completely about all of this. If I can get a message to just a few of them, then I can put other plans in motion."

"From what you've told me, I don't think you can trust anybody in Washington. The only ones there that I knew weren't crooks just died on Air Force One."

"I'm afraid a few of them might not have been as trustworthy as we thought. No, it has to be somebody outside of the capital.

Someone who is not a part of the government in any way. Someone from my past. Any thoughts?"

"So many of the people we deal with are not really close friends. I don't know if you could trust them. You can't take a chance. Not business and certainly not government related. Who else is there? You can't tell your pastor about this and put him in danger. What about friends from way back, even when you went to college? You stay in touch with a few of them, don't you?"

"A few. I've lost touch with most of them. But you have just given me a great idea. I know exactly who I can call."

"You do? Who is it?"

"First, I will call the pastor who could get word to the kids so they know we're alive. Then, there's R. J. Burroughs. He's a professor at Wharton. My favorite teacher of all time. I'd trust him with anything."

"How can you get up with him?"

"No one will be suspicious of friends of Azim who live in the States. He'll surely know someone who can help us get up with Dr. Burroughs. I'll get Azim on it while you and I get a bite of food and some clean clothes."

"And you too, darling. You look like you've been out cleaning gutters or something."

"I'll call Azim, now."

8

Dr. Burroughs had just completed his final lecture of the day. As was his routine, he began his short walk across campus down the street to the small independent bookstore just a block away. His limp became more pronounced as the day wore on. In recent months, he had taken to using a cane to relieve the stress on his arthritic hips. He sat at a small table next to the brewing station, fixed himself a straight black cup, and spent an hour reading his favorite business journals. His wife of forty-three years had passed away two years prior, so being home alone was the least favorite part of his day. There were just too many memories on the walls of his small home. The bookstore was always full of young people and other professors where he would occasionally be included in raucous discussions on the issues of the day. He had heard earlier about the crash of Air Force One and was trying to keep an ear tuned to the news as much as possible. It was a considerable loss to him personally to hear of Donald's death. He hadn't spoken to him in years, but considered him a friend all the same. They had established a bond that hadn't weakened though decades of time had passed. He was startled when another old friend, Dr. Mazarat, approached his table. He was also a professor at the University, though not at the Wharton School. They had both taken part in some faculty roundtable discussions over the years and debated one another's opposing ideas quite often.

"May I join you, Dr. Burroughs?"

"Of course, I'd love some company."

Dr. Mazarat was an expert in Middle Eastern archeology. He had lectured recently on the state of several historical treasures that were being desecrated by factions of radical Islamists throughout that region. Dr. Burroughs had attended those lectures and looked forward to an opportunity to talk with him face-to-face on the subject.

"I recently listened to your lecture on the destruction of historical structures in the Middle East and found it fascinating. It's such a tragedy that so many of these sites are being destroyed for no real purpose. It benefits no one, yet tears a huge page out of the world's book of history."

"Yes, it is horrific. I'd love to talk with you at length about that subject, but it will have to be at some other time. I'm actually here on another matter. A matter of far greater importance than the destruction of those artifacts."

"What could be more important that I could help you with?"

"Let's walk outside for a few minutes. You can come right back to your coffee."

Dr. Burroughs was intrigued by the apparent secrecy suggested by the need to step outside. He would have been too suspicious to walk out in the parking lot with a stranger who might have suggested this, but Dr. Mazarat had the highest integrity. This had to be a matter requiring the highest confidentiality. They walked and engaged in some small talked about an approaching line of clouds and the chance of rain later in the evening. When they got to the far end of the parking lot, they stopped and sat at an empty, covered bus stop.

"Goodness, Dr. Mazarat, what pray tell is this all about? You have my curiosity working overtime."

"Listen very carefully. What I'm about to share with you could cost you your life if anyone overheard us. It's a very grave matter of the utmost importance to the country."

"You sound like a narrator on the History Channel."

"I wish it were that innocent. It's not."

Dr. Mazarat again looked around the area before he spoke. Satisfied that they were truly alone and not anywhere near a camera or a microphone, he still spoke in a hushed tone.

"Donald Trump is not dead. Neither is his wife."

"What are you talking about? It's been all over the news. I saw the footage of the crash of Air Force One. It was a total loss. No one could possibly have survived."

"They weren't on Air Force One at the time. They narrowly escaped on a private jet owned by a Yemini businessman and associate he has known for years. He wasn't supposed to survive. The airfield was attacked by insurgents trying to overthrow the government of Yemen that was carefully orchestrated by subversive powers based right here in the United States. It's a part of a major conspiracy network, which has used the military and many institutions to usurp the power of the government away from the people and their elected representatives. They have succeeded thus far. When Donald Trump, an outsider, was elected, he had no idea the network existed and immediately tried to buck them. Almost no one knows of this situation, except those who are part of the conspiracy. When they tried to direct his every movement, he resisted and they wanted him out of the way. That's what happened in Yemen. He survived, thank God. But he needs your help to overcome this dark moment in history. He trusts you and wanted me to ask you to please help him."

"How do you know him?"

"I've never met him. The friend who rescued and evacuated him from Yemen with his plane is also an old friend of mine. He knows I teach at the same University as you and that I would do as he asked me. He is an honorable man and loyal friend to President Trump. Will you help?"

"It's just me. Nobody will miss me when I'm gone. Without even knowing what you want me to do, I'll say yes, I'm in. What does he want me to do?"

"Call in sick at work tomorrow. I'll make the proper excuse for you if you like. You need to head to Columbus, Georgia tonight. I'll help you get ready to go. I have a phone here with me to give you. It's a special type of phone. It's been purchased with a fixed amount of minutes on it and is not traceable to any owner. When you call, it will be answered by a third party and your call will switch from cellular to WiFi. It would be extremely difficult to trace even if they were expecting it."

"That's brilliant!"

"I wish I could take credit for it, but there are far greater minds at work on this than mine. As soon as you get to Columbus, go to the contact list on the phone and look for Azim. The number is already programmed into the phone. That's who you're supposed to call. Someone will instruct you from there. I cannot stress enough that absolutely no one can know anything about what you're doing. Go to your ATM tonight and take out several hundred dollars here in town. That should be enough to get you there, a night in a hotel and back. Other than that, just do what they tell you when they answer the phone. The President is depending on you."

"You know, if anybody else on the planet had come to me with this outlandish scheme, I'd have called the cops. But I know you are a serious person who wouldn't waste my time on such nonsense if it weren't the truth. So, I'll do all I can. Thank you for being willing to take this risk, Dr. Mazarat."

"This is my country too, Dr. Burroughs. Good luck and God bless you. Be careful."

"Count on it."

✳ ✳ ✳

The VFW hall on Victory Drive in Columbus was full as usual. The local band was performing a cover of an Alabama song that was number one on the country charts back in the seventies. Some retired servicemen were sitting quietly at the bar and at the vinyl-topped tables scattered about the room. Conversations had to be loud so they could be heard above the din of music and the other noise in the room. The patrons at any of the tables could be exchanged among any other table in the room and not miss a beat in any of the conversations. The banter universally revolved around their time on active duty, combat missions that had ended decades earlier and some exaggerated recollections of their involvement in these battles. Many of the older soldiers had done little more than push papers in a supply tent. But if that tent was located near a war zone, then they suddenly became General Patton. A few of those in the bar had seen plenty of intense combat time. They had participated in vicious firefights in thick jungles, hidden quietly in muddy rice paddies as the enemy walked just yards away looking for them. They had jumped out of planes at night watching live fire coming up to meet them as they fell, driven down roads in the Middle East littered with wrecked vehicles. Some were the victims of improvised explosive devices planted all along the way. One member spent time rotting in a POW camp in Cambodia and others still wore their war mementoes in the form of prosthetic legs or missing arms. The ones who had participated the least liked to talk about those days the most. Those who had seen the worst parts of wartime usually talked the least. For the latter, they generally surrounded themselves with others who had experienced the same horrendous sights, sounds and smells of war. They were open with each other but it was a tight-knit circle. These men were extremely patriotic to their core. They held their country in the highest esteem and were very much in despair over where their beloved nation was headed under recent administrations. Retired Command Sergeant-Major Bill Little took a sip from his large mug of draft porter and expounded to the small group at his table. He was five foot five tall and five foot wide. Though in his seventies, he was still strong as an ox. A man who'd take no crap from anyone. He'd fought in Vietnam, Grenada and the Middle East. He was not a person you'd want to get on the wrong side of if you wanted to live out your natural life. Most of the men at his table had seen it all. They didn't need to exaggerate about their wartime experiences. Most people wouldn't want to hear a detailed account of what they had been through.

"We took an oath, didn't we? We swore to uphold the Constitution against all enemies, foreign and domestic. Domestic means the corrupt cowards in Washington that have made a career out of destroying the country. Know what I think would work? Stick with me now. I think it would be great if during halftime at the next football game at RFK stadium, they rolled up the turf and dug a huge hole in the ground. Then lined up and shot all of those SOBs in the government, pushed them in the hole, rolled the turf back out and played the second half of the football game. We'd all be so much better off. And, it would be fun to watch."

Many heads nodded in agreement at the table. T. J. Woods sat across from Bill. He raised his beer mug to greet another friend coming toward their table from behind Bill. It was Jim Grimshaw, the retired Ranger and the father of West Point cadet, Jimmy.

"Grimshaw, you old dog. Where have you been hiding? It's been a week since you've been to the hall. We thought you might be out of town or something."

"Just had a lot on my mind. A lot to think about. I really needed to get up with you guys, though. Need to run a few things past you."

"Well, go ahead. What's on your mind? You got a table of experts here on 'most every subject."

"This is serious. I need to have your undivided attention for a couple of hours."

Bill responded, "I don't have that long right now. My wife is expecting me to pick her up from our daughter's house in thirty minutes. Can we get together a little later?"

"What I was thinking is this, let's meet here tomorrow morning 0900."

"They ain't even open then."

"I know, we'll just meet here. I'll pick you guys up. I'll have some fishing gear with me and we'll go to the lake and drop a line in the water while we talk. It's important. Real important."

"And if I don't like to fish? I mean, it's pretty boring stuff to me."

"Just be here. I'll tell you more tomorrow."

"OK, OK. I'll be here. I'll bring some beer."

Morning came early for Jim Grimshaw. He had placed the call to the White House as requested in the note from Jimmy several days earlier, but still had no response. First, he was told that the President was not in and he'd be given the message that Francis Marion had called him. Unfortunately, the message didn't appear to be related to government business and was placed in the stack of dozens of 'please call' messages the President received daily at the White House. Before Donald had an opportunity to look through the large pile of phone messages, the trip to Yemen took him away from the office. News of the destruction of Air Force One slammed Jim in the face so hard, he could barely think straight. He immediately surmised that those running the coup had arranged for him to be killed. His years in the Army, especially in combat, always had him assuming anything of this nature had to be related to some sort of action by a corrupt government. They couldn't be trusted. They had no one's back but their own. With his fishing gear in hand, he walked from the garage of his small patio home to the trunk of his car. Fishing was not the real purpose of this trip, but he wanted it to look real just in case prying eyes were watching. Ever observant, he couldn't help but notice the sedan parked across the street with Pennsylvania license plates. There was one white-haired man at the wheel looking toward him with more than a passing interest. He walked back to the garage and waited a couple of minutes. Carefully, he looked out one of the small windows at the top of the garage door. The passenger from the sedan was still watching to see what was going on at his house. Realizing that time was short and his friends would be waiting at the VFW hall, he decided to go to his car, start heading out and see if the car pulled out behind him. He didn't have to wait long to get his answer. As he walked to the car, the older man got out of his and walked over to meet him.

"Can I help you, pal? You seem to have an interest in what I'm doing over here. Just to let you know, I live here. I'm not shaking down someone's garage, you know."

"I'm looking for someone and I wonder if you can help me."

"Depends. Who are you looking for?"

"I'm looking for a gentleman named Francis Marion. Would you know him?"

Jim was stunned for a moment. This was totally unexpected and caught him off guard. His mind tried to determine if this would be an ally or someone to be concerned about. His appearance certainly didn't appear to be anything close to a government type.

"I might know who he is. Who are you?"

"My name is Burroughs. I'm a professor at the Wharton School. That's part of the University of Pennsylvania. I have a message for Mr. Marion."

"OK. I'll bite. I know him. At least that's a name I'm sometimes called. I was given that nickname by a man in Washington, D.C. Would you know who that person was?"

"I would. It was in a message you received from your son, Jimmy. It was given to him by the President."

"OK, so you're legit. What do you need from me? I've heard what happened to the President. I expect it was done intentionally by domestic enemies inside the capital. What can be done now? It's too late to help him."

"Not really. The truth is, he's alive. He and the First Lady escaped on a different plane that was at the same airport. It was a private jet that belonged to a friend of his who was also with him in Yemen. They're both safe and in Dubai. At least for the moment."

"That's incredible! Incredible and wonderful news. But I heard on the news this morning they're going to swear in the Vice President as the new President later today. What's going to happen? What do you want me to do?"

"I don't know much more than you. My contact from the Middle East told me to contact you personally to remind you that you may be under full surveillance and to stand by. You will be contacted under the same pseudonym. Here's a non-traceable cell phone. The President and those helping him have this number. They use a WiFi system to call you so there's no record of a phone call. When the time is right, you'll get a call. They want you to have some trusted men at your disposal, maybe as many as fifty. They have to be experienced combat veterans that you would trust with the most sensitive intelligence information. Gather them up and stand by. Listen to the news and be prepared to act when you are called. It won't be long now, so be ready. You'll have your instructions prior to taking any actions. Just collect enough men and be ready to act when needed."

"It's strange that you showed up this morning. I was just headed to meet some fellas I knew from Vietnam. I was going to feel them out about helping me when the time came. I guess that time is here. If you speak to your contact again, you can relay to President Trump that I will have some men who can be trusted and who are ready and willing to lay down their lives for their country once more."

"I will. And Major Grimshaw."

"Yes?"

"It's an honor to meet you. It gives me hope to see there are still real men like you out there who can be counted on to come to the aid of their country."

"You don't have to thank me. My country means everything to me."

"I can tell. Well, I am headed back to Pennsylvania. It's a long ride and I heard on the news I might be heading into some snow."

"Be careful. Thanks for all you've done."

Fifteen minutes later, Jim pulled up in front of the VFW. As expected, his three friends were already there waiting on him. They piled into his car.

"Sorry I'm a few minutes late. I had a visitor this morning and it was important that I spoke with him before we had this meeting."

"This is a meeting? I thought we were going fishing."

"I don't even like fishing and I don't eat fish. This is a meeting. Going fishing was just an excuse."

"Why do we need an excuse? What are we doing wrong? I'm too old to go drinking or to a strip club or something. It took me and the old lady thirty years to declare peace at home and I ain't doing nothing to break the treaty."

"It's nothing like that."

Jim pulled out of the VFW parking lot and talked as he drove up Victory Drive.

"What I'm about to tell you is a matter of highest national security. I've asked you guys to meet with me for two reasons. You spent most of your adult life at war, and I know you can be trusted. I'd trust you with my life. In fact, that's what I'm doing right now."

Bill Little carped, "For crying out loud, Jim. This sounds like we're in a briefing tent before heading into the boonies to look for Charley. Are you sending us on a secret mission? What're you up to?"

Jim continued, "I know you all have heard the President and the First Lady were killed when Air Force Once was shot down in Yemen."

"We did. Stinkin' towelheads. Need to nuke the whole area. They've been at war for two thousand years over there and probably will be for another two thousand if the world survives. So, yeah, we heard. What about it?"

"They're not dead. They escaped on a private jet and are hiding out in another country."

"Hiding out from who? Why don't they just call Uncle Sam and get another jet over there to pick them up? How do you know all this?"

"The problem is they're hiding out from some very bad folks who are in charge on the inside of the U.S. government."

T. J. Woods, interjected, "Let me get this straight. The Commander-in-Chief is hiding out from our U.S. military?"

"You remember when President Trump visited West Point and I told you my son Jimmy served as a cadet escort?"

All of Jim's companions muttered, "Yeah."

"Donald Trump passed him a note that said there had been a coup and the military was running the show. He and the First Lady are basically prisoners. He told Jimmy to get the message to me because my boy told him I was a retired Ranger. He figured he'd take the gamble that we weren't part of what's going on and that we'd help if he asked us. A guy came by early this morning with another message from the President. He is getting ready to make his move against the traitors who've taken over. I'm on board and I'll do whatever I can. Can I count on you guys to be with me? I'm going to need about fifty guys we can trust completely to be with us when the time comes. I don't have a clue about what he expects a bunch of old soldiers to be able to do, but I'm sure I'll know more before the time comes. I do need to know that you're with me on this. Don't forget, you can't so much as breathe a word of this to anyone. They're going to be watching and listening for any sign of a threat and there are cameras virtually everywhere these days. Just be yourselves until you hear more from me. What do you say?"

Bill Little volunteered without hesitation, "Hell yeah! I'm getting tired of sitting around the VFW drinking beer and talking about how it was way back when. I'm ready for some real action. Who wants to live to be an old man anyway? How about you two?"

Bill looked over to T. J. and Ed Young. They both gave him the thumbs up sign.

"That does it, Jim. You've got the start of your new Ranger platoon right here. We'll wait to take action until you give us the word. Meanwhile, I think I need to lose a few pounds and get back in shape. I'm too fat to fit into my fatigues. Hell yeah, I'm ready!"

"Thanks, guys. Now we need to go to the lake and do some fishing. At least let's drop our lines in the water and have a few beers to make this excursion look legit. I have to tell you, I'm glad I got the call. This is the most alive I've felt in twenty years."

✷ ✷ ✷

The Situation Room was full. Vice President Snowden and General Morrison sat next to each other at the end of the conference table. Younger officers and Secret Service agents with their lapel mics crackling swarmed about like locusts. The monitors decorating the walls were broadcasting images from every possible camera throughout the White House and the Capitol. Morrison was a stickler for details and this day was going to be full of highly technical logistics.

He turned to Snowden. "OK, this is your day to take the oath. You need to look and act the part. You have some kind words to say about Trump?"

"I'll have everyone in tears before I'm through. This reminds me a lot of when you and I were junior officers together back eons ago. Who would have thought we'd end up here running the entire world?"

"I did. To tell the truth, I wouldn't have settled for less. You sure you're ready?"

"I'm sure. Relax. Nobody's firing back at us. This will be a walk in the park."

"Just don't forget who really runs this show, soldier. You and I are just hired help."

"I know my job. I'll take care of it. Don't worry about it."

Lieutenant Drexler walked over to Morrison. "General, there is a phone call for you coming in to the room just now."

"It's going to have to wait until the swearing in is over with. I have too much going on here for the next several hours to handle any calls. Even emergencies will have to wait. Got that?"

"I do, sir, but I think you're going to want to take this one. You need to speak to this person."

"Is that right? Who is it?"

"It's Donald Trump, sir. At least that's who he claims to be and it certainly sounds like him."

A look of absolute bewilderment came across Morrison's face.

"I'll take it privately. Clear the room. Snowden, you stay here."

In ten seconds, the room was empty. Morrison went over to the black desk phone and punched the button underneath the flashing light. He slowly raised the receiver to his ear.

"This is General Claiborne Morrison. With whom am I speaking?"

"I'm sure you recognize my voice, General. It's Donald Trump. President Donald Trump. I'm willing to bet you didn't think you'd be hearing from me today. I'm sure you must have heard about my plane being shot down and all. Many folks probably think I'm dead. You did, didn't you? But no, I'm still here. I'm sure the Vice President will be relieved. He certainly was in over his head as Vice President and I know he couldn't have been looking forward to moving up another notch. You can break the news to him that he won't be needed to fill in for me."

"Where are you calling from?"

"That didn't take long. I'm really not sure, general. Somewhere in a land far, far away from anything you have any control over. And don't waste your time tracking the call. It's not traceable. Don't you worry about arranging my transportation back home. I'll make the arrangements from here. Oh and I am going to alert the media of my return to the U.S. so don't waste your time on little details like that either. After all, you have a conspiracy to run. Right? Talk with you again soon. You can count on it."

Morrison slammed his fist against the polished mahogany table. He stared at the ceiling a full minute with his arms crossed until he was able to compose himself. He realized the implications of what had just happened. Donald Trump was alive and none of his own people were covering him. It seemed that everything he had been working for could come unraveled. If that occurred, it would mean Leavenworth for him and many others who were willing participants in the power grab they had orchestrated. He would stop Trump no matter what it took. The military and Secret Service had a great many assets and he would use them all to bring this to a halt. He started his emergency plan, actions that needed to be undertaken immediately. He called his staff back into the room.

"Donald Trump is alive. I want to know what planes took off from the airport at Yemen just before and after Air Force One was destroyed. Who did they belong to? Where did they come from, and where did they go? Get up with our contacts working with the rebels and tell them we need the air traffic controllers' log if it's still intact. Talk with other control towers and any of our air bases that could have picked up that flight on radar. If a taped transcript exists, get a copy of it pronto. I want at least two AWACs in the region monitoring all traffic headed toward the United States. Contact TSA and tell them they need to check in with their counterparts in the Middle East and look for any activity that might be used to get Trump back over here on a plane. He's not going to remain where he is for long. He knows Snowden is waiting in the wings to be sworn in. He'll make some kind of notice to the media today in an attempt to stop that from happening. We have a carrier group in the Persian Gulf and at least two fighter wings. Put them on high alert."

Lieutenant Drexler needed some clarification of these rapid-fire orders. "On alert for what? We don't know whether he'll use a military plane, a commercial airliner or even a small private plane. Maybe even a boat or a ship just to clear out of the area. I don't know what to tell these support groups to do."

"It's certain with the time factor he's under, Trump will use a plane. He had to have help from someone wealthy enough to own a private jet. Check out who might have been visiting Hadi in Yemen. Also, look at any friends or business associates Trump might have in that part of the world. There was that Arab guy he was friends with back in school. Check him out. People won't quickly risk their own life and take on the U.S. military. I'd bet he was well acquainted with whoever flew him out of Yemen. And there's another thing we need to do right here at home. Contact our people watching his kids. Pick them up, no matter where they are or what they're doing and bring them here. They could be just the bargaining chip we need to get Trump to come to his senses. He'd have been better off to hide out on some remote island and just remain dead. Now, we've got to make certain he actually is deceased."

✷ ✷ ✷

The Trump kids were devastated by the news of their parents' horrific deaths in Yemen. Eric took Tiffany and Barron to stay with friends outside of the capital until all the details regarding the crash of Air Force One could be determined and arrangements were made for the memorial services. Donald Jr. and Ivanka stayed behind in New York monitoring the media for any updates. It was a very emotional time for them all. After two solid hours of tears and consoling one another, they had pulled themselves together enough to call for a car to drive them to the local parish where they could speak with their pastor. Donald always worshipped there and enjoyed sermons from his favorite pastor, Jason Frye. They had called earlier to arrange for a private meeting with him to go over a planned memorial service that would be held for their parents. They knew Donald would have wanted Jason to conduct the service and deliver the eulogy. As the limousine pulled up in front of the church, Pastor Frye was already outside waiting for them. Ivanka ran over to him and sobbed into his shoulder as he hugged her.

"I'm so sorry, Ivanka. This has shaken me to the core as well. It was so unexpected. I don't know what to say. Donald, you and Ivanka come inside where we can talk about this tragedy and decide what needs to be done. Come with me."

The Secret Service guards were instructed to never let the younger Trumps out of their sight or earshot. They followed closely. The old stone church was empty as they entered. Their footsteps sounded eerily loud on the slate floors. The pastor led them to the front of the chapel and seated them on the front row. The altar was just behind Pastor Frye. He politely asked the two Secret Service guards to sit three rows back.

"Ivanka is very upset, as I'm sure you're aware. Could you please give her a little privacy so I can say a prayer with them?"

Ivanka was sobbing loudly and Donald was constantly dabbing his eyes with a tissue. The last thing either of them ever thought they would be doing today would be making arrangements for a funeral service for their father and stepmother. It was surreal. Pastor Frye came over directly in front of them and knelt down. He placed one hand each on the outside shoulders of both of the young Trumps. He announced the prayer loud enough to let the guards know so they might show some respect for the moment.

"Let us pray. Father, be with Ivanka and Donald during this time of great loss. Help us to understand that the timing of our birth and death is not in our hands, but in yours. Be with them and give them comfort in their time of need. Guide them toward strengthening their faith and grant them peace in the knowledge that they will be reunited with their parents in eternal life. We ask all these things in the name of Jesus Christ. Amen."

He then leaned over close to Ivanka and Donald. He whispered so softly it was barely audible, "Ivanka, please sob a little louder. I don't want the guards to hear me."

Ivanka complied with his request. The guards were ready to move back a couple of rows so they didn't have to listen to such a massive outpouring of grief.

Pastor Frye continued. "Listen to me carefully. Your parents are not dead. There was an attempt to murder them, but it was not by the rebels, as most people believe. They were both rescued and are safe in the Middle East with close friends. They are planning to return to the United States shortly, but it has to be carefully planned. They want you kept away from any Secret Service or military. Your Dad thinks some conspirators will try to hold you hostage so he won't speak out against the people who tried to kill him. Get a message to Eric and alert him to take Tiffany and Barron somewhere away from all of this and stay out of sight until it's over. When I get up, you start crying loudly and act as if you're going to pass out. Donald, I'll direct you to take your sister to the restroom through the chapel door to your right. Get up quickly and I'll distract the guards. I can't do that for long. The outside door will be just beyond the restrooms; my car is the black two-door. The keys are in it. Get away from here as quickly as you can. Don't stop for anything. Stay on the back roads and head for Columbus, Georgia. There's a slip of paper on the car console with a phone number and the name Francis Marion on it. Call him the minute you get to Columbus. I'm going to get up now. You ready?"

Ivanka nodded her head as she cried ever louder. Jason stood up and held out his hands as if asking her to rise up. As she stood, she began to cry ever louder, sobbing into her brother's shoulder and then slumping as if she would fall over backwards if he weren't holding her up.

"Jason, she's about to faint. Where's the restroom?"

"Just through the door to your right. Get her a wet towel and cool her off. If she doesn't get control soon, I'm afraid we'll need to call an ambulance. She may need some medical treatment and sedatives to get through this difficult time."

Pastor Frye walked back toward the guards as Donald helped Ivanka struggle to stand and stumble through the side door. The moment they were through the door and it closed behind them, they picked up their pace and went quickly to the waiting car.

Jason continued to speak to the guards in an effort to buy some time for their escape. "If she doesn't settle down in just a minute, you'll either need to call her an ambulance or drive her to a hospital. Can you men take care of that?"

"Yes, sir, pastor. We'll give her a couple of minutes."

To Jason Frye, the two minutes passed like two hours. One of the guards finally looked at his watch. A muted phone buzzing could be heard coming from the pocket of the other guard.

Pastor Frye looked at him and asked. "Can you take that outside please? We don't allow cell phone use here in the chapel. It's something we don't want to let get started. Please."

The guard walked briskly to the front door of the chapel and hit the answer button as he cleared the door. Lieutenant Drexler was on the other end of the call.

"Williams, General Morrison says to bring the Trumps to his office in the Pentagon immediately. They are with you, aren't they?"

"Yes, sir. I mean we're at church with them. I stepped outside to take this call. She's sick and in the restroom with her brother.

She might need to go to the hospital first. I'm not sure. What should I do if she's sick? You want me to just bring the brother?"

"Listen carefully. Bring them both to General Morrison with no stops and do it this minute. Got it?"

"Yes, sir. We're on it."

Williams opened the large wooden chapel door and ran up to the front of the room where Pastor Frye was still talking with the other guard. By now, Donald and Ivanka had a good ten-minute head start on making good their escape. Williams looked directly in Jason Frye's eyes and there was something there that told him that things were not as straightforward as he believed.

"Pastor, where are they? Where did they go?"

"They're still in the bathroom, I guess. Just through the door there."

Williams ran out through the chapel door and stopped in front of the door marked 'Ladies'. He pounded roughly on the door, fearing the worst.

"Ivanka. Donald. Are you in there? You need to come out right now. We have to go. Come out! Do you hear me?"

With no response after five seconds, he pushed open the door and entered to find the room completely deserted. Now, having difficulty taking in enough air to even speak, he said to Pastor Frye, "Where did they go? If you don't speak up now, you're under arrest and you can answer that question in front of the Director of the Secret Service."

With a smile on his face, Jason Frye answered, "I want an attorney. I do not wish to answer any questions without the presence of my attorney."

The two Secret Service guards understood they had failed dramatically in their one assignment, to keep the Trumps under their control at all times. This could be the end of their careers and quite possibly a lot worse.

"You'll need to come with us, pastor."

"Certainly, young man. Lead the way."

9

It was late in the evening. Donald sat with Azim in the suite at the top of his office tower. The lights of Dubai danced outside the large windows and bounced off the Persian Gulf in the background. The day had been long and Donald was wracking his mind to come up with a workable plan to go after Morrison and the rest of the conspirators back home. His biggest problem was to determine just whom and how many people were involved. What departments did they actually control? How much influence did they have over the national media? There was certainly a degree of involvement from many areas and contacting the wrong person within any agency or department could mean an instant bad conclusion to his plan. It had to be foolproof in every way.

"You know, Azim, Morrison may have control over the mainstream media, but I'm willing to bet some of the smaller local stations don't have a clue. They would never take the chance of exposing their operation to hundreds of small radio and television stations all over the country. Eventually, somebody would blow the whistle and draw unwanted attention their way. I think I can put together a taped message with my photo attached, perhaps holding up a newspaper headline saying I was killed. That would establish that I'm alive and show that it was taken after the crash.

But what else could I tell them that would generate the right sort of heat on the conspirators? That's the question. I need to find a way to get back into the U.S. without tipping them off that I'm back or who's working with me. If it's all right with you, I'd like to leave Melania here where she's safe."

"Absolutely, Donald. She should stay here. She'll be safe. I'll see to it personally."

"Thank you, Azim. Without your help, we'd already be dead and the country would be lost."

✳ ✳ ✳

At three p.m., the evening news staff was gathered in the break room of Channel 13 in Kansas City, Missouri. Weather person Renee Blakely went to the fax machine. It was her responsibility to get the afternoon meteorological weather fax from the National Weather Service. It gave her a good overall picture of the weather patterns that would be affecting the regional weather for the rest of the evening. Holding her ever-present coffee mug, she reached with the other hand to remove a fax that had come in a few minutes earlier. She was so shaken by what she read, that she lost her grip on the coffee mug. It fell to the floor shattering into a dozen small pieces and spreading a nice covering of black coffee across the room.

"My God! Steve, come look at this."

The evening anchor, Stephen Flynn, was already on his way to assist her in cleaning up the spill. He reached out his hand to grab the fax sheet she was extending to him. She said nothing; she just watched to see his response. The fax contained a photo of President Trump holding up a newspaper with the headline reading, "President Trump and First Lady Dead in Yemen." It was the previous day's headline from the *New York Times* and the date could clearly be seen in the heading. Under the picture was the following caption:

"I'm not dead, neither is the First Lady. We were rescued by a private citizen who flew us out of Yemen to another location that must remain confidential until we are home safe. Rest assured that I will be returning to the United States in the days ahead and will hold accountable those within our own government who aided the Yemen insurgents in their attack on President Hadi's palace and the airport. Your station was chosen for its reputation of high integrity reporting and independence of affiliation with any major national news networks. Please release this story immediately. The entire country will owe you a debt of gratitude. President Donald Trump."

Renee looked at Flynn as she asked him, "Do you think this is legitimate? I mean, could it be PhotoShopped or something like that?"

"I suppose that's possible. Somebody get the super geek in here. Let's see if he thinks it's fake."

Sammy Dobbs was the station's engineer, a self-proclaimed geek. He was extremely competent with anything of a technical nature. His lanky frame, shoulder-length hair, and two weeks' worth of unshaven face were a dead giveaway that his job description at the station included the words 'behind the camera.' He walked over to where Stephen Flynn was waiting, fax in hand.

"OK, Sammy what do you think? Real or fake?"

"Let me get my magnifying glass and a bright light so I can check it out. You need to look at the edge of the individual pixels to see if the transitions are smooth and natural. If it's been 'shopped,' you can clearly see the rough edges where it's been pieced together. Give me a minute to check it out."

Stephen explained to the rest of the crew what was contained in the fax. The room was electric by the time Sammy returned with the answer.

"I think there's better than an eighty percent chance it's real, and I am pretty good at this. I don't see any red flags to indicate otherwise."

"Unbelievable. What's the consensus? Do we run with it or not?"

The room was unanimous in its decision. David Mathers, the station's senior news anchor, joined the discussion.

"You know I have a lot of faith in Sammy's ability to judge these matters. If this is real, then this could be one of the most important events in United States history."

Stephen had to ask, "Why would we be the ones to get this? Do you think we were the only station in the entire country this was sent to?"

"Take it at face value. He obviously doesn't trust the major news networks. He thinks they may be in bed with whoever the conspirators are within this country. We're small, we don't play ball with the big networks, and we tell it like it is. I don't see how we can do anything but report it. If I were running this show, I'd lead off with it. We'd be foolish to start running it past every news agency and government office first. I can tell you what they'll do. They'll just put us on the map the way they did Roswell, New Mexico. They'll guarantee everyone that it's not real and we've been smoking the wacky weed."

"I have to agree with what you say, David. I also think it's real. We'll put it out there at six p.m. Then hold on for the hurricane that will come right after it."

"You can count on that."

The six p.m. producer of the evening news cued the cameras and pointed at the anchor.

"Good evening. I'm Stephen Flynn and this is the six o'clock news. We have a breaking story this evening that you will only find on this channel. We'll get to that in just a moment, but for now let's go back two days. We covered the tragedy involving Air Force One and the death of President Donald Trump and First Lady Melania Trump. A large number of the President's staff and entourage were also reported killed in that explosion. Tonight we have confirmed breaking news that the Trumps did not die in the crash. Our sources tell us that they escaped in a private aircraft that was also at the airport at the time of the attack. Our source for this breaking news? The President himself. We received this fax late this afternoon. We have a close-up of that fax on the screen right now. We have not received any follow-up to this fax at this time, but we had our experts look over this document. They believe it to be genuine. As you can see in the photo, President Trump is holding the *New York Times* article showing the headline speaking of the downing of Air Force One. You can also clearly see the date in the upper corner. We are sending out copies of this fax to other agencies throughout the country and will break into our regular programming to bring you any updates or developments on this story as it unfolds. Let's go now to our senior political analyst for his thoughts on this story."

Within seconds of the completion of the story, the phones in the studio began to ring off the hook. The firestorm was underway.

✱ ✱ ✱

General Morrison held a copy of the fax in his hand. He was seated in the leader's office with three other generals and numerous government officials. With over twenty high-profile individuals present from the world of government and business, the room looked like a gathering spot for many of the best-known, well-connected people in the country. They were deathly quiet as they listened to Morrison explain to the leader.

"They apparently did escape unharmed in a second plane. We have people on the ground over there and our tech crew is looking at data from the internet, phone records, emails, personal phone logs and many other sources to track down where they are and how they managed to pull this off. Our entire fleet around the world is on alert. There are at least two dozen fighter jets available. I can't stress enough that if they return to the States in anything other than a body bag, we're in deep trouble. It's one thing to be shot out of the sky by terrorists in the Middle East. If they turn up here alive, it would be impossible to stage another random tragedy that would be believable, especially after this."

He slapped the fax against his other hand. "He's smart. He went to a small news station in the Midwest and gave them an exclusive. Trust me. It'll be on every news outlet in the world within the next hour. We've got to act fast if we're going to be able to put a stop to this."

Their leader nodded to the general directing him to sit.

"I think you can see where we're at with this. If Donald Trump makes it back to the States alive, sixty years of planning and work will be destroyed. All of you will be in federal prison, some waiting to be executed for treason. The stakes couldn't be any higher. I want you to find Trump and his wife. Wherever they are, on the ground, in the air or even aboard a ship. They must be eliminated within the next twenty-four hours. General, do whatever you have to. No excuses are acceptable and none will be tolerated. Do I make myself clear?"

"Yes, sir."

General Morrison and a small convoy of his senior-ranking officers, the other Joint Chiefs, and his personal aides sped through the city back to his private office in the Pentagon. After briefing his subordinates with the marching orders to 'get the Trumps,' Morrison screamed at the men to get on it. No one would eat or sleep until the Trumps were dead.

He then turned to his aide, "Drexler, you stay with me. The rest of you get out of here and get this started. Now!"

Morrison turned to his Lieutenant. "Where's the pastor?"

"He's being held in the next room."

"Nobody saw you bring him in?"

"Just the guard at the parking tunnel driving under the building."

"Bring him in here."

"Yes, sir."

Jason Frye came into the room. He was carefully watched by the two agents who had brought him in, but he was not wearing any sort of restraints. Morrison stared at him with steely eyes and a scowl on his face.

"I'm sorry, pastor, but I don't have time to make nice with you. You've helped two individuals escape from protective custody. In their current state of mind, they're subject to say or do something that could harm a great many patriots."

The pastor showed no hint of fear as he replied, "I know what you are and what you're doing, General. You've sold out your country for a little bit of power and now it's about to collapse around you. You don't need to tell me you're sorry. You had better start making peace with your Creator because you're going to be visiting him very soon. You'll undoubtedly have a lot to answer for."

"That may be so, but that's a long way down the road. You need to be more concerned about the here and now."

"You don't frighten me, General. The world is full of small people struggling to steal power. You're just another despot about to fail."

"Think what you want, pastor. We have some questions that you're going to answer for us whether you want to or not."

"Oh, you're going to waterboard me, huh?"

"That will seem like a refreshing break in the ocean compared to what you're going to experience. We don't have time to take half measures. None of that is actually necessary if you'll tell me what I want to know right up front. You do that and I'll have someone escort you back to your church quickly."

"Why don't I believe you? You seem like such an honorable person."

"A pastor and a smartass in one package. OK, have it your way, pastor."

Morrison turned to Secret Service agent Williams. He handed him a printed list on a half sheet of paper.

"These are questions that the good pastor will answer, and quickly. Do you understand, Agent Williams?"

"I do."

"Take him to the interrogation room. I'll have a team waiting for you."

Morrison looked at Jason Frye one last time and said, "Sorry, pastor. This was completely your choice. Not mine."

"I'm reminded of Pontius Pilot, General. And don't worry about me. I'm not the one you should be seeking to forgive you. Your problems are far greater than mine."

"Get him out of here. When you have the answers, bring them to me."

✱ ✱ ✱

Donald and Azim sat side by side as they addressed trusted associates and friends of Azim's. Most had known and worked with him for years. They all understood the power of the enemy with whom they were dealing. There was a distinct danger that anyone might be turned by the right motivation, whether it was a huge financial reward or the threat of death to one of them or their loved ones. Time was short, so that was a risk they would have to accept.

"I don't need to tell any of you the dangerous nature of what we are going to discuss right now. Just being found out as a participant here could cost you or any of us everything we have, including our lives. Tonight you are involved in an attempt to save the free world from tyrants in charge of the most powerful military in the history of the world. If they're not stopped soon, they will control every government and all of us. I'm willing to take the chance we can do something to stop them. I hope you are with me. If you want to leave now, I understand. I just pray that you will remain totally silent about what we're discussing here. That's the least I would ask of you. Does anyone need to be excused?"

They all knew the risk they were taking, and everyone stayed.

Donald addressed them. "I thank you for being here. In a few days, the entire world will know what you did and they will thank you also. Azim and I haven't had a great deal of time to come up with a plan, but we have done our best. We've already taken some steps. We have sent substantial proof to a small TV station in the U.S. that my wife and I are alive. I'm sure they immediately broadcast the story. Undoubtedly, stations under the control of the conspiracy leaders will be labeling the story a bad hoax and trying to discredit it. Of course, the only way that will hold water is if I never make it back to the United States. The conspirators will stop at nothing to prevent me from returning. Sadly, their efforts will be with the full cooperation of the infiltrated U.S. military and the intelligence agencies. It would shock you all to know how much they are continuously monitoring communications and activities around the world. They will discover in a short time whose plane we rode on to escape from Yemen and track it here. It could literally be any minute that they break through these doors." Donald pointed toward the conference room doors as he spoke.

"I have to start my journey back home this evening. Before that can take place, my wife needs to be protected over here somewhere safe, at least somewhere not under the U.S. control. Any thoughts?"

An older associate raised his hand as he spoke. "I'm Mohammed Hassan. I came from a very tiny village in Qatar many years ago. I have family there that I trust. It's primitive, but safe. I can get your wife there with friends, and she will be protected. There is no monitoring possible there as there are no power lines, no television, nothing modern. They raise goats mostly. Would this be acceptable?"

"It sounds like exactly what we need. We are very grateful for your help. However, do not underestimate the intelligence agencies. If they get any hint at all that she might be in such a place, they will fly unmanned aircraft above your heads. You will not be able to see or hear them, yet they can take pictures of the tiniest wrinkles on your face from miles away. She must be kept inside until this is all over."

"I understand. It will be done."

"I will tell the First Lady goodbye right after we are through here. You should take her to your village as soon as possible."

"It will be as you say. We leave the moment she is ready."

"That's one big item handled. Next, we need to figure out how to get me back to the United States. I don't think the military forces of any country should be involved. The tentacles of the Pentagon are long and intertwined throughout the world. Who would have thought they were working with the insurgents in Yemen? Azim, any thoughts on how to make the trip which stands a decent chance of succeeding? It has to be underway tonight."

"I've been thinking about it constantly. I believe I have a workable plan."

"That's good news. What are your thoughts?"

"My first thought is that they will be looking for you and the First Lady traveling together so splitting you up is a good start. Second, every major airport, train or bus station, cruise ship terminal anywhere in the Middle East will be looking for you. With the new facial recognition software and cameras everywhere, it would be next to impossible to get you aboard any commercial carrier. I can work around all of that."

"Really, how will it work?"

"First let me ask you, Donald. How do you look in black?"

✽ ✽ ✽

Jim Grimshaw had finished his initial meeting with the group of retired Rangers and retreated to the kitchen of his mother's house. He was trying to keep the conversation to just small talk and not give any hint of a problem in their discussion. The phone rang in the kitchen. Millie casually picked it up and listened quietly for a moment. She walked over to Jim, receiver in hand.

"It's for you. Please take it outside as I have a headache."

Jim was confused at her sudden announcement of a headache.

"I'm sorry, you should have told me. I could come back later. Can I get you something for it? Aspirin, Tylenol, anything?"

"No, that damned old washing machine started leaking again today and just thinking about it has given me a headache. Please take the call outside so I don't have to listen. You're so deaf from all those years of jumping out of noisy airplanes and cannons going off in Vietnam that you yell like Francis, the talking mule."

Mildred put extra emphasis on the name Francis as she spoke. The confused look on Jim's face suddenly disappeared. He clearly understood her message. He walked out to the center of the backyard and put the phone to his ear.

"Yes."

"Are you Francis Marion?"

"I am."

"I'm Donald Trump Jr., President Trump's son. I'm in Columbus with my sister Ivanka. We were given your number to call. There are people after us. The same people that tried to kill our parents. Will you help us?"

"Don't read any street or business names. What do you see when you look around?"

"We're at a park along the river that has many rapids. There's a bridge to our right, a tire store across the street, and a diner of some kind."

"Be on the lookout for my brown pickup truck. I'll drive around the park and I'll be by myself with a John Deere ball cap on. Be there in ten minutes or less. If anything starts to look suspicious, bail out and call me again later. Got it?"

"Yes."

"I'm on my way."

In less than five minutes, Jim was at the park. As he made his first circle, he saw a small dark car flash its headlights. He drove slowly toward it until he could see that there was a young couple seated in it. He pulled alongside and rolled down his window. Donald Jr. lowered his as well.

"I'm Francis Marion. Actually, Jim Grimshaw. I'm here to help you. You can't leave that car here, so follow me. Don't get too close. I don't want to draw any attention. I'm going to make a few calls to some folks on our team and we'll get you both to a safe place until we figure out what has to be done. Your father's people are in touch with us and we're getting messages from them just like you did. We're here for you. Let's get out of here."

The two vehicles left slowly and disappeared outside of the city.

✱ ✱ ✱

Deep inside the Pentagon, General Morrison and his key staff members poured over maps of the Middle East. Eliminating the threat of Donald Trump and the First Lady re-entering the country would be simple if they could locate them. They had many associates throughout the Middle East who would be only too glad to be of assistance for the good will it would buy them from the U.S. military. However, they were finding it very difficult to pick up on the whereabouts of Trump and whoever was helping him. Across the room, a young soldier read a decoded note that had just come into the room.

"Yes! General Morrison, sir, over here."

The general quickly moved over next to him.

"We've found the plane, sir. At least we know who it belongs to. It's a private jet, just as you thought it would be. It took off less than four minutes after Air Force One exploded. One of our bases went through their radar tapes and picked it up. It headed out toward Dubai. The owner of the jet is from there. The plane is owned by a corporation named Persian Hotels. The president of that company is a guy named Abdul Azim. We have people looking for where the plane is kept right now."

"That's great news, son. If I'm not mistaken, that's the guy who was a friend of Trump's back in college. Makes perfect sense. We need to locate that plane, ASAP!"

Morrison called out to Lieutenant Drexler, "Get me our station chief in Dubai. Do it yesterday."

✳ ✳ ✳

Azim stood in the small private hangar talking with three other men. One was dressed in a business suit, the second in the traditional Arab taub and the third in a dark black flight suit. In an unusual move, the pilot was wearing a military style flight suit instead of the normal uniform he wore as Azim's private pilot. He was holding a free-fall parachute.

Azim spoke directly to him, "The pick-up vessel will be waiting for you one hundred miles out. You have the exact coordinates?"

"Yes, sir. When I pick them up, I'll set the aircraft on autopilot aimed straight out to sea at top speed. I'll drop out of the plane directly over the boat and have my hand-held VHF radio with me. I'll direct them to me in the water. They will blink a small light until I see them. They'll pick me up and we'll head back to the coast in the dark. We should all be dispersed before sunrise."

"You are very brave. Your parents should be proud of the man they raised."

"Thank you, sir. I need to get under way immediately."

"May Allah be with you."

The entire process of opening the hangar door and taxiing the plane outside was done in complete darkness. The pilot finally cut on some running lights as he neared the end of the taxi lane. He turned the sleek jet around at the end of the runway. With no other planes waiting in front of him, he went full throttle and was airborne in just seconds.

Azim turned to the two other men. "Thank you both for your help. I will not forget how you have helped with this brave act. We must leave now, as quickly as possible. What we have done here must remain completely confidential. Our lives and our families' lives will depend on it."

The men shook hands with Azim then quickly departed. Less than five minutes after they left the airport, a convoy of six dark sedans and SUVs sped onto the airport property and parked outside of the now empty hangar. The door was once again tightly shut, but Western music could be heard coming from inside. Realizing that there must be maintenance personnel working inside, they quietly surrounded the building and coordinated their forced entrance through two small side doors. They were metal doors and locked. Not wanting to launch an all-out attack on the building, one of the men leading the group banged on the door. With no answer, it was repeated several times. Still with no response, the order was given and a small explosive was placed on one of the doors. It was blown completely off its hinges by the force of the explosion. Once the portal was open, agents with guns drawn entered the dark and empty space. A small green light was apparent on a tool bench toward the back of the room. An agent went to the light source to discover it was generated by a small boom-box type of stereo playing rock music from an American CD. It had been strategically left in that fashion to do exactly what it had accomplished. It bought a few minutes for the plane to make good its escape. One of the men placed a call to their superiors and alerted them there was no plane in the hangar. An immediate jaunt to the control tower revealed to them that the plane normally in that hangar had departed about fifteen minutes prior. Entirely unaware of the scheme, the tower supervisor offered them the plane's identification numbers, which he stated were plainly inscribed on the wing. The information was quickly relayed through two sets of cooperating stations to General Morrison.

He took the phone from a subordinate and explained his orders in no uncertain terms. "Bring down that plane. It must be stopped at all costs. It threatens the United States if it reaches any of our coast or territories. This is a national emergency. Stop that plane."

Morrison handed the phone back to the young soldier. He turned to Drexler. "It's just a matter of time. With a twenty-minute head start, a squadron of F16s will intercept it in short order. Bring up the monitor and let's see the radar path of our aircraft. Is there an AWAC up there?"

"Yes, sir. It's hoping to pick up a track from the enemy aircraft to give our fighters a heading. Right now they're flying on a straight course toward the States. Here they are on radar."

The large monitor showed a flight pattern of five F16s in a tight formation flying at a high rate of speed. There was nothing showing on the screen in front of them yet. Morrison looked at the radar blips with keen interest. It was something he had witnessed many times before during his long-standing military career.

He directed the engineer controlling the monitor. "Can you bring up the flight crew communications, please?"

"Of course, sir."

The initial communications were basic. Air speed, directions and pattern controls. Then came the much anticipated call from an AWAC plane monitoring flights in the suspect area.

"We have radar contact with a single craft, definitely civilian, maintaining over four hundred knots. That speed puts it in the class of the type aircraft we're looking for. Trajectory corresponds properly for leaving Dubai and heading to the States. I don't know what fuel capacity this plane has but to reach the States under normal circumstances would be highly unlikely. It's continuing to maintain that course, however. Your call, Eagle Team Leader."

"Roger, Sky-eye. We're going to pay a visit to the suspect aircraft. Flight Leader to ground control, we will be approaching at six hundred knots retaining our formation. This is the only aircraft in the region. This must be our bird. We'll be back with you upon reaching target."

"Roger, Eagle Team Leader. We have you on ground control radar."

The pilot of the private jet had also spent considerable time in military aircraft. He realized fully that he would have the most sophisticated fighter jets in the world on his tail in only a matter of minutes. He monitored his global positioning satellite screen constantly. When he reached the designated drop zone, he could pass by it so quickly that it would be difficult for him to drop down close to the fishing vessel assigned to pick him up. At four hundred plus knots, he would need to time his evacuation from the jet precisely. It would take a few seconds to open the plane's cabin door and make good his escape. The flight crew had pre-rigged the door so that all he had to do was unlatch it and it would literally fall off the plane. The latch and the door's seal were all that were holding it in place. He counted down the longitude and latitude flashing across the screen. He could see a waypoint clearly marked against the lighted background. The jet was approaching it at a phenomenal speed. He was at the controls of one of the fastest private aircraft manufactured anywhere in the world. It was not supersonic but it approached that threshold very closely. When he realized it was time to make his move, he made certain the course the plane was set on would continue on autopilot until the tailing aircraft shot it down or it ran out of fuel. He quickly moved to the cabin door, secured his oxygen mask and pulled the latch down watching the door fly off in less than a second. He again checked his oxygen mask to make certain it was properly attached over his face as the jet had been pressurized for high altitude. Bailing out at that height would be fatal without it. He shrugged his shoulders to make certain his chute was nestled properly and then fell forward out of the aircraft. He tumbled three times head over heels until he gained control of his descent. He would hold off pulling his chute's release ripcord until he was less than a thousand feet from the ocean. Opening it higher would allow for more drift caused by the strong ocean breeze that could pull him away from the boat he desperately needed to reach. He wanted no part of spending the night on the ocean's surface waiting for things that were already swimming in it to realize he was there. He pulled his chute and just a couple of minutes later landed in the dark ocean. He immediately released the lines, and slipped out of the parachute harness that held him to the chute. He grabbed at a flashlight in a shoulder holster. After removing it, he secured its thin retaining cord around his wrist. He pushed the light's switch into the on position and was relieved to see a strong beam of light emitted from the end of it. He did a three hundred and sixty degree turn in the water with the light shining as far out as he could aim it. Overhead and far away, he could hear the sound of jet engines screaming in his direction. He quickly turned off the flashlight. He looked up into the black night sky and watched as the lights aboard the squadron of F16s passed directly over his head. They were moving at a high rate of speed and he was relieved that he had reached his rendezvous spot when he did. Another few minutes and his fall to the sea would undoubtedly have been in what was left of the cockpit of his plane as the pieces fell around him into the dark waters. He continued turning in circles and shining his light for fifteen minutes. When he saw a light flash on in reply to his own, he felt an adrenalin rush unlike any before. In mere minutes, he was aboard the fishing boat assigned to retrieve him.

Fifteen minutes later, the team of F16s could see the suspected jet on their radar screens but nothing was appearing in the dark sky ahead.

"This is Eagle Team Leader. We are closing on the suspect target. We are two thousand yards out. Our course and target's course are synched. The target is not attempting any evasive maneuvers. We are within range, but cannot get a visual on the target. Target is flying lights out, completely dark. Not even wing lights. No strobes, nothing."

Morrison was trying to suppress a smile. He spoke directly to the F16 Team Leader in an unmistakably clear voice. "This is General Morrison, JCS."

All those monitoring understand that meant ground control command. "That has to be the target we're after. You are to eliminate that target immediately. Make certain with visuals that you see it destroyed. Do you copy?"

"Roger. We will engage momentarily."

The radar screen clearly showed the F16s in a tight pattern directly behind another aircraft and maintaining a perfectly straight course. Any modern jet would have sounded a radar alarm that an aircraft was approaching from the rear but there was no communication attempt of any kind being made at this time. No evasive maneuvers. Even the F16 Team Leader thought it was like a runaway train with no engineer aboard.

"This is Eagle Team Leader. I'll take the first go at the target. I am locked on. Rockets are under my control, ready to launch. Missiles underway."

Even on the radar monitor in Morrison's office, the missile trail could clearly be seen moving up quickly to the small jet that was their target. There was a sudden flash on the monitor and the leading jet disappeared from the radar screen. The Team Leader broke off from the formation and banked steeply so he could visually watch as debris from the jet fell back into the black ocean.

"Ground control, JCS, this is Eagle Team Leader. Target has been eliminated, no recovery possible. I have visual of the craft striking the ocean. There is fire on the surface."

"Very good job, Eagle Team Leader. I don't have to remind you, this is to be considered top secret by you and your entire team, including ground crew and AWACs support."

"Roger, this is Eagle Team Leader. Formation returning to base."

General Morrison was on fire with gloat. He had proven that with his keen military intellect and decades of experience, any lesser individual would not be a threat. He would make short work of any attempt to thwart his directions. Three hundred miles ahead of the F16 team, a sixty-foot fishing vessel was steaming back into the port. The pilot of Azim's downed jet was already out of his flight suit, dried off, and sitting in the bridge of the old wooden fishing vessel. It was a traditional fishing trawler just like dozens of others plying these same waters that evening. It was so inconspicuous in its appearance that no one would ever suspect it of being involved in the high stakes game of world politics in which it had just participated. In two hours, it would be safely back in port offloading its cargo. Fifteen hundred pounds of fish and one hundred eighty pounds of aviator. The captain, two crew members and their guest stared into the dark waters ahead of them, satisfied with mission accomplished.

✸ ✸ ✸

That same evening, simultaneously with the takeoff of Azim's jet, another faction of Donald's support team had been undertaking an equally dangerous move they hoped would lead to Donald's safe return to the States. Azim had explained to Donald and several associates who would be taking part in this alternate portion of the scheme how it was designed to work.

"My jet will be taking off in the next few minutes. I'll be headed to the hangar right after we're finished here. I want to personally thank the pilot who volunteered for this very dangerous mission. Undoubtedly, the U.S. military, who don't have a clue who General Morrison and company are really after, will be trying to track it. Morrison knows you will be trying to get back as quickly as possible. Once they realize my plane is gone, they'll have their target and go after it. That should allow us time to get you out of here safely. By the way, is that burka comfortable?"

"If you can't recognize me under it, then it's comfortable. So, what's the plan?"

"We're going to put you aboard a fishing boat. It's in a crowded part of the wharf where no one will ever think something like this would happen. We probably have a couple of hours' head start. If they destroy my plane and check the wreckage, they'll be very disappointed to find no bodies. Then, the chase will start again. By that time, you will have off-loaded to a large yacht, which will meet the fishing boat about fifteen miles out in the Gulf. You'll continue with them for about twenty-five miles and move to a third, larger boat. That boat has a fast helicopter aboard. They'll fly you to meet a private jet on an island off the coast of North Africa. One more transfer to a small charter jet that will take you to the island of St. Martin in the Caribbean Sea. The last leg of your journey home will be aboard a large yacht from St. Martin to the coast of Georgia where a workboat, a fishing boat I'm told, will take you to shore. There your friend, Francis Marion, will meet you. If all goes as planned, you will be there late tomorrow night. From there, the plan becomes all yours. We will get you there; that's a promise. Whatever you do, do not speak. Arabic women are not expected to join in conversations with men, so it will not seem out of place. Just keep a low profile. It's time now. Let's get you to the dock and onto the fishing boat."

"I'm ready, Azim. When this is all over, I'll be back. Then we will have some pleasant time together, like we did in college."

"Those were good days, my friend. I'll hold you to that. May Allah be with you."

"Thanks."

10

Grimshaw entered the VFW canteen bar. He was confident that Ivanka and Donald Trump Jr. were safely tucked away at Milt Conner's hunting lodge. Also a retired Special Forces-Ranger, Milt had been a close friend for many years. The group he had been assembling had now swelled to over twenty. Selecting retired Rangers and Special Forces veterans to join was tricky at best. They had to be one hundred percent reliable with enough strength and vitality left to be of help if things got difficult. As easily as war stories circulated at every VFW hall, Jim's main concern was that only those directly involved with the plan would ever hear about it. Maintaining complete secrecy would be difficult even though he didn't question the integrity of the great majority of the veterans. Walter Edge was tending bar. Walt and Jim had been friends since high school. Both had joined the Army, and served several tours in Vietnam together. Their bond was undeniable. They absolutely knew they had each other's back. Jim was using him as a point of contact at the VFW for everyone whose help he'd enlisted. Walt couldn't even approach anyone if there was the slightest reason to think they might not be willing to come aboard or might blow the whistle on what they were doing. Too many lives depended on it.

Jim leaned over the bar and whispered, "Walt, they're safe in the country. I'm going to head out that way late this evening or first thing in the morning. A couple of guys are coming in to see me about the job. I need to speak with them before I can leave."

"They're already here, Jim. Farthest table in the back corner. Red ball cap on one, hunting vest on the other. I know them both. You won't go wrong with them."

Several seats down from Jim in the nearly deserted bar, William Davis sat in a near drunken stupor. He was a veteran that had been overtaken by the bottle in recent years. This was his new battlefield, and he was losing the fight. He saw Jim and thought he might get him to have a beer with him. Many of the other vets wouldn't have much to do with someone who was drunk most of the time.

"Jim, how you doing, man?"

"Good, Willie. How about you?"

"I'm OK. Spend a little too much time here at the bar I guess. Can I buy you a beer, old friend?"

"Not right now, Willie. I'm meeting some other guys here I have to talk with. Maybe later."

"Bring 'em over. I'll buy them a drink too."

"No can do, Willie. We're talking business."

"Business? Here? What kind of business?"

"I'm just trying to buy a new truck. Something I can use to go hunting that won't get stuck out in the woods. Need something with a little more weight, you know?"

Willie was almost falling off the stool as spoke. "You can borrow my old truck any time, pal. It never gets stuck."

"Thanks, I'll sure remember that."

"Great, Jim. Have fun hunting. How 'bout bringing me another beer, Walt? I'm running low on fuel."

Jim walked over to the corner table. After a brief conversation with the two men seated there, he walked outside by himself. Five minutes later, they left as well. They had arranged to meet beyond the reach of anyone who might try to listen in.

By eleven p.m., the VFW canteen bar was practically deserted. Several tables had one or two guys drinking their last round of the night. At the bar, there was no one but Willie. He had no idea how many beers he had consumed. The only one counting beers was Walt, the bartender. He was starting to wrap things up for the evening. It was always a chore to chase out the last few serious drinkers who had no place to go where anyone was waiting for them. Left to their own devices, they would live on their bar stools.

Walt yelled out, "Let's wrap it up guys. I'm closing down in five minutes."

Willie asked, "Is there time for one more beer, Walt? You know, one for the road."

"Sorry, Willie. That's it for tonight. Do you have a ride home? You're in no shape to be driving."

Willie was just starting to answer when the front door opened and two young men in suits walked in. They surveyed the place. Seeing it was almost empty, they walked over to Walt who was still behind the bar.

"Good evening, fellas. We're about to close here. You need a quick beer before you leave? I could stay a little while longer."

"No, sir. We're looking for someone. Thought we might find him here."

"Who would that be?"

"Mr. James Grimshaw. You know him?"

"Yes I do. I'll see him tomorrow and be glad to tell him you were here looking for him. Who should I tell him was trying to get up with him?"

One agent opened his wallet and produced an identification card. He flashed it to Walter.

"Secret Service, huh? You trying to recruit old Jim for a job with you spooks?"

"We just need to talk with him. Do you know where we could find him right now?"

Willie, who was three sheets to the wind and close enough to hear the conversation, unexpectedly blurted out through his stupor, "Jim's bought a new truck and heading out to old Milt's hunting lodge to try and get it stuck. That's what he said."

The agents seized on this information, as they knew it was coming from someone too drunk to lie.

"Old Milt?"

"Yeah, Milt Conners. 'Bout fifteen miles up in Harris County, next to where Slater's Mill Road dead ends. Can't miss it. Big old red barn where you turn in."

Realizing that Willie had just given away the hiding place for the Trump kids, Walt said, "He's drunk. He's talking about Wilkerson's Quarry up at West Point Lake. That's where the best bass fishing in the county is. You need to get on out of here, Willie. You're going send these fellas out on a wild goose chase in the middle of the night."

"Oh, I ain't that drunk, Walter. I know where the hunting lodge is. Been there a million times."

"Without any further conversation, the two agents turned and ran out of the hall."

Walter looked at Willie. "You damn drunk. You've just sicced the authorities on Jim, you old fool."

"Sorry, Walter. I was just trying to help."

"You can help by getting out of here. Right now! Git!"

"All right, all right already."

Willie slowly descended from his stool and stumbled out the door.

Walter cleared everyone else out within a minute and locked the door behind them. He found his cell phone under the bar and called Jim's number. There was no answer. Jim had turned his ringer off and left the phone in his truck while he talked with the two men he had met at the VFW. They were several miles outside of town in the middle of a freshly plowed field. After being assured of their help, Jim had made his way back to the truck. He never checked the phone for missed calls.

Walter tried twice more to get him on the phone, but Jim never turned the ringer back on. It was late and he was tired, but felt he needed to check on the guys at the lodge. There was too much on the line to take anything for granted. Walter ran to his car and headed to the lodge. He thought he might have a chance to get there before the agents if they made any sort of stop or missed a turn on the way.

That didn't happen. The agents had immediately entered Slater's Mill Road into their GPS and gone straight to the end of the road, finding the red barn just as Willie had described.

"Quarry, huh? The bartender was trying to shut him up. This must be our place. The information they got from the pastor was right on target. We pick up the Trumps and our careers are made. I'll turn off the headlights so we can ease down this dirt road. If there's a lodge, they'll have some kind of lights burning inside."

"They've probably got a few guards with weapons too if I had to bet. They said these guys were radical rightwing nuts. Paramilitary types."

"I'm expecting that. OK, just ahead. See the light over to the right?"

"That has to be it. Let's park here and see if we can move closer without anyone noticing. I hope they don't have dogs. A gather many hunting lodges have dogs. I don't like the thought of having a bunch of dogs after me. I think it would be a good idea to get some backup out here. I'm going to call for some support."

"Fine. Then let's just shut up and wait."

Within ten minutes, the agent's requested backup was directly overhead. A solid black helicopter descended into a freshly plowed cornfield right beside their position.

The unmistakable sound of a chopper overhead was immediately apparent to the three men inside protecting the Trumps. Milt doused the lights in the small cabin. It was an old farmhouse that was not up to code to be anyone's home, but it made a great spot for a bunch of old friends to meet. They would gather there, open a bottle of whiskey, and tell war stories before heading out early on a hunt. It did have a basement with a walkout at the back of the house and a hidden entrance under a filthy old rug in the hallway. Realizing they would soon have company, Milt told his two buddies, Alan Burns and Lou Matthews, to hide the Trumps out of harm's way.

"Guys, get them into the basement. Do it quick. Visitors are going to be here any second."

Alan pulled up the rug and handed a flashlight to Donald Jr.

"Quickly, you need to stay down there no matter what. They may not realize there's even a space underground here. Don't use the light unless you absolutely have to. Ignore whatever you hear up top. Don't make any noise until we come for you. If we don't show up, then stay quiet until morning and then try to slip away into the woods. Grimshaw knows we're here. He'll come find you."

Donald Jr. looked at the men. "You know they won't hesitate to shoot you, don't you?"

"Trust me, we've all been shot at a lot during our lives. We're still here. Getting rid of us ain't gonna be easy. You can count on that. Now, you both lay low 'til this is over."

As soon as they were down the steps, Alan shut the trap door behind them and threw the rug back over it. Milt saw flashlights moving down the road outside and approaching the cabin.

"Here they come. Alan, you take the window over to the right. I have the other side. Lou, you take the back side all by yourself. You both got plenty of ammo?"

The men looked at the hunting rifles propped up against the back of the moth-eaten couch in front of them. They each retrieved one and made certain there was a round in the chamber. Lou smiled as he pulled back the bolt to chamber the round.

"This brings back a lot of memories. There's at least a dozen boxes of shells for these rifles. They ain't M16s but a 30/06 ain't a bad gun. It'll do a number on somebody. OK, I guess we're as ready as we're going to be. It's their move."

After several minutes of staring out the corner of the lodge windows trying to stay out of view and yet see what was going on, a bright floodlight illuminated the front of the lodge.

One of the agents spoke through a handheld megaphone. "You in the cabin. This is the United States Secret Service. You are illegally holding two hostages. They must be released immediately. As family members of the President, it is our responsibility to protect them. Holding them in this manner is kidnapping, a class A-1 felony. You must release them at once."

Lou whispered to the others, "Should we respond?"

Milt turned toward him. "I don't think so. I only know that they're not here to protect anybody. The kids get turned over and we're three armed criminals killed while trying to kidnap the President's family. You can count on that. They'll try for a while to get us to give them up without a fight. That's not going to happen. I ain't gonna say nothing right now. The sooner we say no, the quicker they come after us. Let 'em sweat it out a while. They don't want to get shot at either. Tell you what, Lou. You see that floodlight they're hitting us with?"

"Yeah."

"Let them make the first move. The second they make a move toward us, you shoot out the light then move to the back room. Al, you and I can take out the first two of 'em when Lou hits the light. Let's do it all in two seconds."

"No problem."

Fifteen tense minutes went by. The agents tried to get a comment from the men in the cabin with no success. The novice agent on the scene was eager to see some action as opposed to just looking fierce while holding a radio. He eagerly offered his opinion on the situation to the senior agent. "Look, these are just some old retired Army has-beens. They've probably spent the last twenty years sitting on a barstool, drinking liquor and crawling back to their trucks. Let's just go take 'em out."

"You have a lot to learn. Most of these guys spent years getting shot at on a daily basis. Some of them are retired Army Rangers, Special Forces and infantrymen. If you think we can just waltz in there and they're going to roll over for us, you're dreaming. They know what they're doing. This can get real nasty in a hurry. Keep your gun in its holster until I tell you to take it out. This doesn't need to get started 'til we're ready."

Six more men came running up after exiting their chopper. Two were Secret Service wearing dark clothes. The remainder wore combat fatigues and helmets wired with microphones so everyone could hear what was being said. The senior agent approached the two younger men while crouching down to avoid becoming a target.

"I'm McCarthy. What's the situation here?"

"We tracked these guys here from the VFW hall in town. They have Trump's kids and aren't responding in any way. I'm sure they're all retired military. "

"How many are there?"

"Three, four, maybe more. Some could have already been there when the others arrived. I'm betting they're heavily armed. It's a hunting lodge."

"You've tried to get them to talk with you?"

"Yes. No answers of any kind. There was a light inside when we first got here, but that went out first thing."

"OK. Try one last time to get them to answer you. If they don't, then we have to just take the place down."

"What about the Trumps? If we open fire, there's a good chance they might get hit or even killed."

"We didn't do it. The kidnappers did it when we tried to save them. Nothing we could do to save them. Understand?"

"I think so."

"Good. Now give 'em this message. They have two minutes to release the Trumps, come out and throw down their weapons.

Otherwise, we're going to have to take action against them. Tell them this is the last offer to end this peacefully."

The agent picked up the megaphone once more and offered the men one last chance. They still gave no response. Milt, Lou and Alan each had their gun sights trained on what was to be their first target. When the two minutes had passed, McCarthy turned to his group. "Positions everyone. On my order. Three, two, one, fire."

Before the crack of the first bullet firing had ended, the spotlight they had trained on the house went dark. It literally exploded in the hand of agent controlling its beam. One helmeted soldier who had gotten off a single round and the eager young agent both fell straight over to the ground. Both had terminal wounds from direct hits. The Rangers' shots had been spot-on kill shots. Less than five seconds into the fray, two of their men were dead. With the lights out and no visible targets to shoot at, the vets in the lodge stopped shooting after the first three shots found their targets. McCarthy ordered the rest to pull back and get behind their vehicles for cover. Though extensively trained for the jobs they held, none of the agents or the soldiers assisting them had ever experienced real-life combat. It was nothing like a swat team breaking into a house with a single scared felon waiting inside. This was a entirely different scenario and McCarthy knew it.

"We're going to need more backup. If we stay out here within their range, they'll pick us off one by one. We'll just lay back and wait until we can get superior numbers of men and firepower here. We're going to need an ambulance as well. Are either of our guys alive?"

One of the soldiers shook his head letting him know they were not breathing. McCarthy picked up the microphone to the closed channel radio in the chopper and requested immediate help. He turned to the other agents.

"It could be as much as an hour before we get more support out here. Maybe less, but I doubt it. Just stay out of range and lay low until they get here."

Inside the cabin, Alan crawled on his belly back over to the basement door. He opened it only slightly and spoke in a hushed voice to the Trumps. "You OK down there?"

"We thought we heard gunfire up there? Are you all right? What's going on?"

"There are five or six guys out there. Most are Secret Service with a few army backups from the chopper. They started it and they got a little more than they bargained for. They backed away and I'm sure they have more folks on the way. We're going to stay put and hope some of our guys get here before things get worse."

Walter came to the turn at Slater's Mill Road. There were blue lights flashing across the intersection and he could make out at least three State Highway Patrol cars. Officers were standing outside of their cars with flashlights in hand stopping any traffic that might show up. At this time of night, anyone driving out that way would be considered suspicious. He killed his lights and pulled over to the side of the road. He could hear at least one helicopter heading in the direction of the hunting cabin. He knew there were only three guys inside unless Grimshaw had gotten there ahead of him. It was apparent the government agents realized the Trumps were there. The agents and their forces would be gathering enough firepower and support to make sure they wound up on the winning side of whatever happened. Three men against dozens of armed agents and soldiers, even three old Rangers, would not have much of a chance. He knew he couldn't do anything to help them by himself, so he turned the truck around and started back toward town. If he could find Jim, they might be able to figure something out before it was too late.

Within thirty minutes, Secret Service and Federal agents were swarming all over the hunting lodge property. They were relieved by the fact that it was located by itself so many miles out in the country. There were no witnesses to what was going on. They could have the final word on what happened there. McCarthy received a call from General Morrison.

"McCarthy, listen carefully. I want the Trumps alive. They're no good to any of us dead. Donald Trump won't take any action if we're holding his kids. But if they don't survive what's about to happen, you just make sure the people in that cabin are to blame for it. Understand?"

"I do, sir."

McCarthy called about half a dozen of the Feds together. "We've got our marching orders. We overpower these rightwing wackos and if the Trumps get hurt in the process, make sure we're in no way taking responsibility for it. OK, once our people are completely surrounding the cabin and you're ready, give me a call on the walkies. We might as well end this ASAP. Let's get on with it."

Within five minutes, McCarthy had the go-ahead from every group. He grabbed the walkie again.

"On my count. Three, two, one."

The night air suddenly came alive with rifle shots and small explosions. Inside, Milt, Alan and Lou were fully expecting the attack. They held back on returning fire and lay against the cabin floor with water soaked towels over their heads. Though they all realized fully what they were up against, their words belied any hint of fear. Milt spoke just loud enough for his friends to hear him without giving any information to the forces outside.

"Boys, we're dealing with a bunch of rank amateurs here. They've shot out all the windows and the smoke grenade is blowing out as quickly as it went off. Stay low and be quiet. Wait until they think we're out cold and they start moving closer.. Then, pick out your targets and hit 'em back hard."

Another command went out over the handheld radios, "Cease fire."

McCarthy, realizing no one was returning fire, assumed they were either unable to breathe from the smoke and already passed out or had somehow left the cabin before it had been surrounded.

"Group leaders, each of you send a couple of men to both sides of the cabin. Use caution. One of them might still be conscious."

They had no idea just how conscious they were. As they got within twenty feet of the cabin, Milt gave the signal to return fire. Each man picked out a shadow moving toward the cabin and fired a single shot each. Within seconds, three more agents were on the ground with severe wounds. They were screaming and writhing in pain, begging for help. The remainder of their force wisely made no move toward the men lying on the ground. It was becoming clearer by the second just how deadly the men in the cabin could be. The shots from the Rangers hit their marks dead on. With only three shots fired in this round, they had taken a dramatic toll on their enemy.

Milt told his friends, "OK, hold back again. I think they're about five minutes out from giving us everything they've got. I don't think they'll be doing any more reconnaissance missions to see if we're still alive. They've got the picture pretty clear by now."

Alan laughed softly and replied, "Who would've thought we'd go out fighting against our own troops?"

Lou added, "These ain't our boys. Remember the oath. Against all enemies, foreign and domestic. These are the domestic enemies. They're much more dangerous than the foreign kind 'cause nobody suspects 'em. They're a bunch of weak-kneed, limp-wristed, chicken shit Secret Service creeps. Never trusted them. They ain't nothing but hired guns for whoever manages to get in control of Washington. I'm good with making my stand right here. I want to go out fighting for something worthwhile. You can't beat this. We have the rightful President's kids in the basement. They better come at us with all they got or the whole lot of them will be looking up at stars or down at dirt."

"Amen."

The minutes ticked by like hours. They could hear a loud motor firing up outside. Milt had a good idea what it was.

"Here they come. Bet they're using one of those armored SWAT vehicles. They'll have about a half dozen men inside and six or more men following it for protection. That means they'll all be coming at us from the same direction. The ones out back won't make any move without cover. They'll just be watching to see if we try to slip out the back. They'll come right up to the front of the cabin. Might even try to crash through it. Let's move to the back room. When they come in the front, take out as many as you can as quickly as you can."

Lou looked at his rifle. "These bolt actions don't let you get off too many shots in a hurry."

"Just make every shot count. Here they come."

The noise from the armored vehicle grew louder by the second until it sounded as if it was literally over top of them. The driver avoided the front steps and elected, as Milt had guessed, to slam into the side of the building to the left of the door. The building shuddered under the impact. The farmhouse walls were made out of heart pine cut right on the farm and the rigid beams didn't allow the vehicle to penetrate the exterior of the building. The framing cracked and moaned, but didn't give in. The attackers would have no choice but to continue their attack on foot without the cover of the large vehicle. The front door opened and a combined force of about fifteen men began to breach the building through the door and the windows. The Rangers all exercised great discipline, derived from years in actual combat. They offered no resistance until their targets were clearly framed in the doorway and windows. When the troops tried to make good their entry into the cabin, the Rangers simultaneously opened fire. This time, the cabin was completely filled with the fire from multiple weapons firing in every direction. The young soldiers with no combat experience were so rattled by the reality of actual combat and seeing their comrades falling around them, they just pulled the triggers on their automatic weapons and emptied their entire chambers in seconds. The Rangers were still laying low. There was so much smoke in the room, they were almost invisible but they could no longer see the advancing troops. They started aiming at the rifle and automatic weapon reports. More of the troops fell to the floor.

Seeing how badly it was going, McCarthy directed his men, "Fall back and hit them with grenades."

The three Rangers heard the command as well. Milt spoke to his friends, "Good job, guys. They'll be a long time forgetting us. It's been an honor to know you and serve with you. Can't think of any other hill I'd rather be on right now."

His buddies responded in kind. Four seconds later, the entire structure was obliterated when multiple grenades exploded throughout the structure. McCarthy thought this would certainly be the end for the Trumps as well.

He told his men, "When the smoke clears, check it out. No way anybody survived that. Find the criminals first. Make sure they're not breathing. Then get our guys out of there. Nobody gets left behind. Right? Then find the Trumps' bodies and bag 'em. General Morrison wants them delivered to him personally and nobody ever says a word about what happened here tonight. Not a word. There will be serious consequences for anybody talking about this."

Twenty minutes later, all the bodies were lying under sheets in the yard. All but the Trumps were accounted for. Very little was left of the interior of the cabin. All of the inside walls were down and debris covered most of the floor. One of the soldiers looking through the rubble stepped over a large beam and plunged straight down the old basement stairway. The steps were gone so he fell a full ten feet to the hard ground of the basement floor.

His right leg suffered a compound fracture and he called out in pain. "Help me, I'm down here. There's a basement."

Spotlights began to light up the cabin. The light also went off in McCarthy's head. "Shine those lights around the basement. See if there's anyone there."

Ivanka and Donald Jr. were soon found huddled together, unharmed in the far corner of the room. The soldier called back to McCarthy, "They're here. They look fine."

"Bring them to me. Take care not to get them hurt in all this rubble."

Ivanka and Donald Jr. were shaken but silent as they were brought before McCarthy. Their faces and clothing were completely black with soot and dirt. They could barely understand what McCarthy was saying due to their ears still ringing from all of the explosions. McCarthy escorted them out of the cabin and onto the front yard. As they walked, they had to step around the sheet-covered bodies that littered the lawn. Donald Jr. could readily see at least fifteen bodies. He also felt that the three men who had tried to save them must be under some of those sheets. They were led over to a waiting SUV and driven away from the scene and on to the nation's capital.

***

Deep in a sound sleep Grimshaw, thought he must be dreaming until the pounding got so intense it brought him back to his senses. There was someone beating on his front door. He slipped on some pants, tucked a 9mm handgun in his belt behind him and cautiously walked over to investigate the source of noise.

"Who is it?"

"Jim, let me in. It's Walt from the VFW. Let me in."

Jim quickly let a distraught Walter inside. Jim took a quick look around outside before he closed the door. Instincts were kicking in and he was starting to perceive a threat from the outside. He was naturally on guard. Walt, though upset, remained calm as he spoke with Jim.

"Feds, they came into the hall. They asked where you were and I told them I didn't know. Willie was there. He was drunk as usual and blurted out that you were headed out to the hunting camp. They turned on a dime and spun gravel on their way out there. I tried to call you several times."

"I think my phone's turned off. I'm sorry, man. I'll get a jacket. We'll go out there and intercept them."

"Far too late. I went on without you. By the time I got there, it looked like the Normandy invasion. Must have been a dozen vehicles, Secret Service, Feds, and Army. They even had the State Highway Patrol blocking the road. I saw two choppers set down. I came here straightaway. We're into something really big. The Feds are all over the place. What the hell should we do?"

"I should have gone out there no matter how late it was. I was planning to, but I was too exhausted to even drive. I was going to go check on everything first thing in the morning. Do you think you were followed?"

"They didn't know who I was. I turned around while I was still pretty far back from the cops."

"Then, the first thing we need to do is get out of here. If they're not outside right now, it won't be long. Trust me. I was the only one in Columbus that had any idea of what's going on with the Trumps so that's undoubtedly how they wound up here. We need to get the word out to the guys I've already contacted to stay on guard and keep quiet. We'll meet some of them at the coast in a few hours."

"The coast? That's a long way from here. Are you talking the Gulf of Mexico down by Pensacola or Panama City?"

"Negative. We're going over toward Brunswick. We've got to pick up a guy heading in from offshore."

"This sounds like something out of James Bond."

"It's a lot harder to believe than that. I'll tell you about it as we drive. I'm going to be counting on you to help me a lot anyway. We need to get out of here right now. There's a lot going on, Walt. Some of it is going to be hard for you to believe."

"I'm with you, Jim. No matter the problem. One thing I know for sure is, you're going to be on the right side of all this. Now, can you tell me a little about what I'm getting messed up in?"

"While we're driving. Got to keep moving."

Jim went to a gun safe in the back of his closet and retrieved several hunting rifles, a couple more pistols and every box of ammo inside. As they exited the room, he remarked, "Thank God for the Second Amendment. If we didn't have any weapons, this would have been over a long time ago."

After several hours of driving and explaining, Jim pulled his truck over to the side of the road next to a large gate that was secured with a length of chain. It was in the middle of a long stretch of back roads with no homes or businesses.

"Where are we, Jim?"

"We're close to the coast. Now, we stand by. I should get a call later tonight or maybe early tomorrow morning. They'll be bringing the President in on a fishing boat. We'll meet them near Brunswick Landing at Valona in McIntosh County. There's some shrimp boat docks there and we should be able to get in and out with no one the wiser."

"I never dreamed I'd ever get to meet the President. And I certainly didn't think I'd meet him under these circumstances."

"Join the club, Walt. Don't underestimate how desperate the turncoats in D.C. are to get him back under their control."

"I saw what was going on back at Milt's hunting lodge. I'm as brave as the next guy, but I don't want to go out like that. I thought when I left Vietnam that nobody would ever be shooting at me again."

"Same here. Let's hope it doesn't come to that."

Jim shut the metal gate behind them and they continued down the dirt road disrupting some startled deer as they approached. After about a mile, Jim stopped the truck.

"Are we there, Jim?"

"Close. We'll stop here 'til we get the call and then move in. God forbid some shrimper comes in while we're waiting there. They don't normally work or dock their boats at night, but I know my luck. So, we'll just sit here and catch a catnap until they call."

Both men were exhausted and still sitting upright in the old truck when they quickly fell asleep.

11

The Superyacht *Iamila* was running at twenty knots through the dark Atlantic. Not many yachts over two hundred feet in length could make sustained voyages at such a speed. It was one of the most beautiful and modern vessels of its size in the world and belonged to a Saudi royal. Custom built in Holland, it offered exclusive upgrades that were rare on most yachts, such as bullet-proof glass in all the exterior windows, well-disguised surface-to-air missiles, and extensive radar to alert the crew of any approaching craft, either by land, sea or air. Prince Asad was in the main bridge of the yacht with his captain, two other deck officers and Donald Trump. Donald had removed the burka that had gotten him through several transfers over the past twenty-four hours. Even though all of these maneuvers had been completed in remote ports and private airport terminals reserved for exclusive clients such as the prince, the United States had eyes and ears on guard throughout most of the world. Nowhere could be considered completely out of their reach. They also understood that all of these resources were now on the highest alert.

"President Trump, do you think it will be safe to go back into your country? You know you are welcome to stay in ours as long as you wish. How do you know whom you can trust?"

"Thank you for your kind offer, Prince Asad, but I must go back to the United States. There are those who are on my side, people of character and morality that can be trusted. They are working as we speak to come up with a plan to go after the conspirators and take back control of our country. This is far more important than me or even my life. The future of the United States and the entire world rests on the prospect of our getting this done. Let me ask you, how many more hours before we arrive?"

The prince interpreted the question for his captain who responded back to him. He then told Donald, "In about four hours, we'll be less than a hundred miles off the coast of Georgia. There will be a local sport fishing boat that will take you from the meeting point in to shore. My understanding is that it will be a high-speed boat and you should be back on land within two hours once you're aboard that vessel. Between then and now, we must avoid the U.S. Coast Guard if at all possible. They are always on the lookout for vessels of all types trying to enter their territorial waters. Presumably, they're after drug smugglers. Right now they must be keeping a sharp eye out for your arrival."

"I'm sure they are."

At one hundred twenty miles from the coast, the captain alerted Prince Asad that a vessel he had been following on radar was now turning in their direction. A few moments later, the running lights of an approaching craft could be seen headed toward them. Several large spotlights erupted from the deck of the approaching vessel and focused on the prince's yacht. The VHF radio clicked on and their vessel was hailed by the United States Coast Guard Cutter *Diligence*.

"Motor yacht directly off our port bow, this is the United States Coast Guard Cutter *Diligence*. What is the name of your vessel? What is your home port and where are you bound?"

"Yes, Coast Guard, this is the yacht *Iamila*. We are an Emirates documented vessel and we are bound for the United States, to the port of Charleston, South Carolina. We are going to enter the Gulf Stream and take advantage of the current there before turning to the North. We wish to clear customs in Charleston."

"Roger, *Iamila*. We would like to board your vessel for inspection."

Monitoring the transmission, Prince Asad asked for the microphone. "Vessel *Diligence*, this is Prince Asad of the Saudi royal family. I assure you if you check with your State Department, you'll find that there's no need to make us go through this inconvenience. My captain tells me the seas are over six feet and there's a good chance you might damage the side of my yacht attempting to board us. Can this wait until we are safely docked in Charleston? Surely you don't think we are smuggling drugs?"

The young captain of *Diligence* realized he now had an issue he had not anticipated.

"Yes, sir. I request your vessel to reduce speed to seven knots and maintain your course until we can make contact with the State Department. That waiver will have to come from them, as we are currently on a special alert for a specific violation. I don't have the authority to grant you a clean entrance without an inspection. Please stand by."

Prince Asad turned to Donald. "Burka time, Donald. I'll also have the ladies aboard surround you in their burkas, so that you don't appear to be the only woman on board. Just remain quiet. I'll do all the talking."

"Thank you, Prince Asad. Please don't risk the lives of your people for me."

"I do this for the world, Donald. The United States President is far greater than the man holding the office. He must be honest and free to do what is right."

"I agree. Where's my burka?"

Twenty minutes later *Diligence* called back on the VHF to let the captain of *Iamila* know that he had been ordered to do the inspection with all due apologies for any inconvenience it might cause. He assured them that it would speed up clearing customs when they arrived in Charleston. The Coast Guard cutter pulled within a hundred yards of *Iamila* and lowered a large ribbed inflatable craft with six men aboard. The Coast Guard crew stood by with lines and fenders to prevent any hull-to-hull contact with the pristine yacht as they approached the lower deck opening on its starboard side. They tied their inflatable craft off to the yacht and stepped aboard. The Coast Guardsmen, or Coasties as many yachtsmen referred to them, were armed with M16 rifles and handguns. The senior officer introduced himself as he spoke to Prince Asad.

"Good evening, sir. I'm Captain Stanley Armstrong. I appreciate you letting us come aboard your yacht and I do apologize for the inconvenience. We are performing a large number of inspections up and down the coast this evening."

"May I ask what for?"

"We have reason to believe there is an immediate threat from both the importation of drugs and even a specific illegal entry. That is basically importing illegal aliens into our country."

"Do a lot of these illegal aliens come into your country on one hundred million dollar yachts?"

"You've got me there, sir. I did call the State Department and they said no exceptions. Otherwise, I certainly would have given you a pass. We'll be as quick as possible. Can you assemble your crew and all additional passengers in one room with their passports?"

"If I must."

Donald was seated in the midst of five women who were also on board. With their faces covered in burkas, it would be hard to distinguish one from another. Realizing the risk involved in discovery, the women gathered into a tight group in the yacht's main lounge. The lights were dimmed just before the Coasties entered the room. Donald was strategically placed toward the middle of the group. Captain Armstrong and another crewmember looked over the group and examined their passports for any sign of impropriety. The prince folded his arms and stared at the captain in an attempt to make him as uncomfortable as possible. He expressed his disdain for this intrusion.

"In my country, our women are revered and protected. They are not put on display for the pleasure of others and certainly never for this sort of government-sponsored parade. Your country should be embarrassed. I realize, Captain, that you are just following orders but I will nonetheless make a formal complaint to your State Department. It could have an impact on the ongoing relations between your nation and mine."

"I understand, sir. Again, this was not my call."

The impatient response and disgust of the prince had its intended effect. The young officer handed the passports back to the prince, much sooner than a closer inspection required.

"All seems to be in order here."

He turned to the women, who spoke not a word. "Very sorry, ladies. I apologize."

The Coast Guard officers left the room and hurried back to the ship's bridge where the remainder of the men had regrouped after inspecting the yacht. Armstrong turned to his subordinate.

"Are we done here? Is everything in order?"

"No problems, sir."

In less than five minutes, the Coast Guard crew was again on their inflatable craft headed back to the *Diligence*. There was palpable relief on the yacht. Donald took off the burka and nodded his thanks to the women. Prince Asad led him back to the bridge where they all watched as the lights on the departing *Diligence* grew dim. Donald took a deep breath and turned to Asad.

"That could have been a disaster."

"Yes, but we are on the side of righteousness. Have faith my friend. You shall prevail."

"I love your confidence, Prince Asad. So, how long before our rendezvous with the fishing boat?"

"That is a question best answered by my captain."

Again, the prince asked the question of his captain and interpreted his reply for Donald. "I'm told we should be meeting the fishing yacht within the next thirty minutes. We have them right here on our AIS screen already."

Donald asked, "What is that screen?"

"It's the Automatic Identification System. Most yachts are equipped with a transponder today that broadcasts who they are, their course, speed and the VHF channel they monitor. See her on the screen? I touch this red number and it brings the information up in a window on the screen. So, the boat we are meeting is

Fancy Fins out of Boca Raton, Florida. They are moving toward us at over twenty-five knots. A very fast boat."

The captain gave commands to his crew to prepare to meet the other vessel for the transfer of their passenger. As the sport fishing boat pulled alongside, the waves were still large. Prince Asad relayed his captain's commands to Donald as he and the fishing vessel's captain both maneuvered their vessels close enough for Donald to leap from one to the other. It was similar to watching a ballet as the two experienced seamen fought to keep the boats close yet apart. Prince Asad reached out and hugged Donald.

"May Allah bless you and keep you safe on this journey, my friend."

"And you also. I will not forget your kindness and the risks you have taken for me and my country."

When the captain of *Iamila* gave the order, Donald jumped into the waiting arms of the captain and crew of *Fancy Fins*.

"Thanks, guys. If you hadn't caught me, I'm afraid I'd have taken a nosedive onto the deck."

"Good evening, Mr. President. Welcome home. I'm Ron Bolan, captain of *Fancy Fins*. Everybody just calls me Ace. The young fellow holding you up there is Winslow. He's my first mate. We're here to take you to meet your contact in Georgia. I think you know him as Francis Marion, hero of the American Revolution."

"Gentlemen, I can't tell you how happy I am to see you tonight."

In the middle of the introductions, they were startled, as *Iamila*'s horn let out two blasts of farewell as the magnificent yacht pulled away. Donald and his new shipmates waved to them in the darkness. Ace looked at his crew and Donald.

"Let's get *Fancy Fins* up to speed. We don't need to be playing chase with the Coast Guard any longer than necessary."

Donald was in agreement with that thought.

"I thought they had us just a short while ago when they came aboard. If they hadn't been so enamored of the yacht, I think they might have conducted a more detailed search. It could have been the end of this little escapade."

As *Fancy Fins* began accelerating across a dark Atlantic, Captain Armstrong on *Diligence* was going over in his mind the inspection of Prince Asad's yacht. It now crossed his mind that the inspection might have been rushed. He called for one of the crewmen who had accompanied him during the boarding.

"Did you look over every single passport while we were on the prince's yacht?"

"Yes, sir. I did. They all looked to be in order. Why, did I do something wrong?"

"It's not that. My question is, how many passports were there?"

"All told, I think there were fourteen. Yes, fourteen. I remember counting them clearly."

"How many of them belonged to the women on board?"

"I had them all together."

The young officer took a moment and began counting in his mind.

"I'm pretty sure that five of them belonged to the women on board. That's correct, five."

"And how many women do you remember sitting in the ship's salon?"

Again, the young man stopped and visualized the women as he counted in his head.

"There were, I'm pretty sure... There were, oh my God, there were six."

"That's what I was thinking as well. Get them on the radio and let's prepare to do another boarding."

The *Diligence* and crew made a turn at high speed as they tried to overtake *Iamila*.

Armstrong called to his ship's navigator, "Do you have her on radar?"

"Yes, sir. She's still headed toward the States. She's made a seventy-five degree turn to the north. Probably just hitting the Gulf Stream since they wanted to take advantage of the current heading to Charleston. She's doing at least twenty-five knots. I'm not sure we can catch up to her."

"Try to get her on the ship's radio. Tell them we have to re-board her. No reason needs to be given. Crap! I can't believe we were that stupid."

"I'm sorry, sir. I should have given the passports back to each person and not the prince."

"It's my fault. I'm responsible for everything that goes on aboard this vessel including inspections. Let's just catch up with her."

Aboard *Iamila*, the captain questioned the prince about their course.

"Sir, why don't we turn back toward home? This will make it too easy for them to keep track of us."

"We will soon enough. We need to give Donald's boat a chance to make shore. If we turn immediately after we said we were headed to Charleston, they'll know it was a ruse. We must play the game just a bit longer so they can make the coast."

The VHF radio clicked on with a call to *Iamila* from *Diligence*.

"*Iamila*, this is the United States Coast Guard Cutter *Diligence*. Do you copy?"

"Roger. This is *Iamila*."

"I'm sorry to inform you that some details of our inspection were overlooked due to our own failure and we will need to re-board you immediately."

Iamila's captain looked over to the prince.

"Tell him that our complaint to his superiors just got much greater in length and severity, but we will stand by until they can catch up to us. How long will it take for them to get here?"

The captain looked over at the radar. "Twenty minutes, maybe thirty."

"Perfect, keep moving a little so that it will take as long as possible for them to catch up. Let's make certain the President has time to get to shore."

Diligence again sent a boarding party over to *Iamila*. After some unpleasantries were exchanged, passports were again collected. The women gathered once again in the ship's salon. Captain Armstrong personally matched up each passport to every woman.

He turned to the prince. "Sir, I'm certain there were six women in here before. I remember it clearly."

"You are mistaken. There were five on board when we left and there are still only five on board. I assure you that none have swum to shore. If you wish, have your men search the entire yacht. My captain will accompany you and your men. When you're satisfied that you are mistaken, come back and we'll see you off. Then, we can complete our journey to America. Of course, after this incident I'm beginning to have second thoughts about even visiting. Apparently things have gone from bad to worse in the

United States. You used to be a very friendly, welcoming country. I don't see that anymore."

"I'm sorry, sir. I'm just doing my job."

An extensive hour-long search of the yacht proved fruitless to Armstrong. He and his crew were confident they had been played for fools, but there was no way to explain exactly how they had been deceived. He would have to make a decision whether or not to mention any of this in his boarding report. An hour after the Coast Guard departed *Iamila* for the second time, the great yacht made another turn and began her journey back across the Atlantic.

12

Grimshaw's phone rang and brought them abruptly out of a coma-like sleep.

"Yeah, this is Francis Marion. What's happening? Yes, we're close by. I can be there in less than ten minutes. We're on the way."

"Was that our guys?"

"Affirmative."

"What's this about Francis Marion?"

"He was a hero of the Revolutionary War. Remember the Swamp Fox?"

"I've heard that name before."

"That's what they call me. I'm sure they know my real name by now, but we did our best to keep it under wraps to keep the feds out of here while we tried to help the President. Can't count on that anymore. I'm concerned that with the technology they have, they could show up anytime. We just have to stay focused and do this quickly."

"What are we supposed to do?"

"They'll be bringing him in to the dock where I'll be waiting for him. I'll give you a couple of quick bursts from my flashlight and you come pick us up in the truck. Got that?"

"Seems pretty simple."

"Let's hope it stays that way. I'm going to go ahead and start walking up there. Remember, two blips from the light."

"I got it."

Jim stood quietly on the run-down shrimp boat dock. Other than a dim yellow bulb burning on the other end of the landing, it was pitch black. He strained to see if he could make out a boat coming up the narrow channel. The night sky and the channel were so black that he wasn't sure how they could possibly navigate through the dark waters.

Ace Bolan was still at the wheel of *Fancy Fins*. He'd been a charter boat skipper off the coast of Georgia for almost forty years and knew the waters leading up to the Valona shrimp dock like the back of his hand. He felt confident he could bring the boat up to the dock blindfolded. As he neared the wharf, he strained to see if anyone was there. With just a brief burst from the boat's spotlight, he could see Jim standing there. He eased the large boat gently up to the wharf. His mate dropped the dock lines over two pilings and Ace killed the motor. Donald stepped out from the boat's cabin and into the cockpit where Ace stood waiting to help him off the boat.

"Mr. President, it's been an honor."

"Ace, your nation is indebted to you. I promise you will hear from me again. I owe you. Ex-military, right?"

"Yes, sir. Navy. Served on the *Hornet* during Vietnam. I'm just glad I could do my part."

"Thanks, again. I better get going."

Donald looked at the man standing alone on the dock.

"Francis, is that you?"

"Yes, it is."

"OK, I'm headed your way."

Donald walked over to Jim and extended his hand.

"It's a privilege, sir."

"If it weren't for men like you willing to risk your life for your country, I wouldn't have made it this far tonight. I'm in awe of your courage."

"I'm Army Special Forces-Ranger, sir. Seems like I've been risking it for years. Just glad I could help. We better get going. It doesn't pay to stay anywhere very long with the folks who are trying to catch up with us. They caught up with three of my friends last night who were looking out for your family. That didn't have a good ending, I'm afraid. All killed."

"I'm sorry. I hate to hear that. Were my kids there with them? Do you know how Donald Jr. and Ivanka are? Are they safe?"

"I've not heard what happened to them. I'm sure somebody will get word to me when it's safe. I'll make some calls while we're under way."

"I'd sure appreciate your finding out whatever you can. I want to get word back to my wife about the kids as soon as I know how they're doing."

Donald gave a brief wave to Ace and the mate as he walked off with Jim. Even before they were out of sight of the dock they heard the engines on *Fancy Fins* firing back up. Captain Bolan didn't want to be at the shrimp boat dock when the crews started arriving for work. No need to raise any suspicion about any unusual activities near the coast. He felt certain there would be people asking questions at every port on the coast over the next couple of days.

Donald turned to Jim. "What's your real name?"

"Grimshaw, sir. Jim Grimshaw."

"It's nice to meet you, Jim. You're Cadet Grimshaw's father?"

"That I am, sir."

"You have a brave, intelligent son! He'll be a good leader."

"Thanks, sir. We need to get going."

"Where are we heading from here?"

"First to my truck and then I'm not really sure. We had to get out of Columbus in a hurry as they were onto us. I'm sure they know we're in this truck. They probably know my license plate number by now. I think we need to keep moving before the sun gets up good, and try to find a safe place we can rest so I can make a few calls. As of now, there are about twenty of us altogether. They're just waiting for the word and a place to meet. I'll get that information to them shortly. First, we need to figure out where that will be and what we've got to do. There is no way a couple dozen old men can take on the military, even if most of them were Rangers. What is your plan from here, sir?"

"The first order of business is for me to make it back to the capital. I have friends and allies who'll help, but there's no way to communicate with anybody that's really safe. They have everything monitored from the telephones to fire hydrants. You wouldn't believe how extensive it is."

"There's not much I wouldn't believe. So, if we can get you back to D.C. with some folks you trust, we're done?"

"That's about all I can think of right now."

"Why don't you just go to the press with this? The public would march on Washington a million strong, if they knew what was going on."

"Some of them are in on it. You let even one of the wrong people know, and they'll stop it so quick you won't have time to blink. One small television station in Kansas has some of the story. They ran it yesterday. If we could find some old fashioned motel off the beaten path where we could rest and watch the news, I'm sure we could come up with a plan. You know, find an old Mom and Pop motel and park the truck out behind it. Can we do that?"

"Sure, let's start there. For the time being, we'll consider that the plan."

Jim flashed his light twice. Ten seconds later, Walt pulled up beside them. They sped off back down the dirt road leading out to the highway. Jim thought the chances of being spotted at night that far from Columbus on a back road would be small. Nonetheless, he and Walt kept a very sharp eye out for suspicious looking vehicles going in any direction. Off to their right, they finally spotted a motel that looked as if it had been sitting in the same spot, unchanged for fifty years. There was an old neon sign reading Oasis Motel that hadn't been lit for decades. The only way to tell it was still in business was the small neon 'open' sign in the tiny office window in the center of the one-story structure. On either side of the office, a row of cinderblock rooms stretched out for ten units each way. From the number of cars in the parking lot, it looked as if three or four rooms were occupied. Walt pulled off the road and Grimshaw hopped out of the truck. The entire staff consisted of the owner and his wife. The wife was sleeping in one of the units that served as their home and the husband was lying awkwardly in a chair next to a desk in the office. Jim found the door to the office locked, so he tapped lightly on the glass with his house key. Startled by the sudden noise, the old man almost fell back in the chair as he quickly awakened and stared toward the stranger at the door.

"What do you want?"

"A room. One room for one night."

"Check-in is at noon tomorrow."

"Just want it for tonight."

"Tonight's almost over. You want a room for just a few hours?"

"That will be perfect. Can you let me in?"

The old man was very leery of opening the door this late at night. He'd dealt with all types over the decades of running this place. Places like the Oasis had become a target for drug addicts and dealers looking for a quick place to get a fix or a cash register to knock over to get money for drugs. He sized Jim up for just a moment and finally let him in.

"Where you from?"

"Columbus. Just getting in. Going to rest up a little, meet some friends tomorrow, and then we're going fishing for a few days."

"That so? How many folks in your party?"

"Three of us will be in the room."

"That's fine. Don't care who does what with whom as long as there ain't no reason for anybody to be calling the law. I don't need to be seeing those folks down here no more this week. Still got crime scene tape up on unit thirteen from the last drug bust. You fellas behave yourselves and everything will be fine. The rooms ain't deluxe, but my old lady keeps 'em clean and they're quiet."

"Sounds great. What do I owe you?"

"Forty bucks cash. Don't do credit cards no more. Bastards want to charge me to let my customers use one. Not going to play that game anymore."

Jim grabbed his wallet and pulled out two twenties. The old man stuffed them quickly into his top shirt pocket.

"Sign my roster here if you would. Law requires me to keep a list. If somebody's got the cash and don't cause no problems, I don't care who they are. Use any name you like. They make me do it."

"No problem."

Jim signed his name John Doe. The old man never even looked at it and handed him a key.

"Unit three, third unit from the far end to your right. You can park right in front. Not much of a parking issue out there."

"That's great. Thanks for letting me wake you up to get a room."

"That's what I'm here for. Goodnight."

Jim turned and walked back to his truck. Walt started the motor and drove in the direction Jim told him. When he got in front of the unit, they decided to pull around the end of the building and park the truck under a live oak tree. It wouldn't be visible from the highway. The room was no better than what they were expecting. Two old beds with mattresses that were sunken into worn-out bedsprings. Tired as they all were, they would have slept in the driveway if that had been their only choice. On the scratched-up dresser across from the beds, there was one old television set. They snickered when they realized it was equipped with rabbit ears for an antenna. Jim went over and turned the set on. After fifteen seconds, it produced a rough picture and he turned the rabbit ears until the reception was good enough to see a clear picture and hear what was being said. He turned the channel knob until he located a narrator reliving the important news of the day.

"Residents in a small community outside of Columbus, Georgia were shocked to hear of a paramilitary group that took on federal marshals trying to serve warrants against their leader for weapons charges. The group of five armed militia members opened fire on the federal agents who were forced to return fire. A spokesman says the marshal's office believes the militants were killed by a fire in the small cabin, which apparently started when their illegal ammo storage dump exploded. The identities of the five bodies found inside will not be released until after the medical examiner can examine their badly burned remains and next of kin are notified. We'll bring you updates as we discover more details about this tragic confrontation."

Jim couldn't control his anger at the lies he was listening to.

"Those sorry bastards! Every word they say is a lie. What's happened to our country? How could such corrupt and immoral individuals wind up running everything? And five militants? There were only three guys there."

Walt nudged him, reminding him that Donald Trump was in the room.

"Jim, they just said there were five people there."

"Oh, God! You don't think they killed the President's kids, do you?"

"I don't know. Why would they say there were five militants? It's the perfect cover for them."

Donald dropped down onto the corner of one of the beds. He stared blankly at the wall across the room, his body trembling with anger and disbelief, tears running down his face. His voice broke as he spoke, "What else could it be? They were guarding my kids. They gave their lives trying to protect them. They die and my kids die. I swear with everything that's holy that everyone involved in this, will pay with their lives. This is the highest degree of treason any nation has ever suffered and they will pay. I swear to God they will pay."

Jim walked over and placed his hand on Donald's shoulder.

"There are still some good men who will take up arms and fight for this country. I'm with you and I know others who will help. You will get revenge and together we'll take back the country."

"How can we overcome so much force and so many corrupt individuals?"

"We cut off the head of the snake."

"I just heard someone else say that."

"It's true. Most people who work for the government aren't evil or corrupt. They're just following orders to keep their jobs. They assume their leaders are straight. Even when they're told to do things they don't understand, they figure they just don't have all the facts that the leaders know. They're trusting in leaders who are lying to them, to everyone. When we get these people to surrender, and we will, the rest will fall in line."

"But with the power they wield, I don't know how we can fight them."

"That's why we're here. Try to get some sleep. Either I or Walt will be keeping watch the rest of the night. One of us will be awake every minute. We'll come up with a plan. I'm getting an idea of just where to go to get the help we need. We can do this. You can count on that."

As worried as they all were, their exhaustion had reached the point that their need for sleep had become overpowering. Donald and Jim each took a bed and laid on top of the blankets still fully clothed. They removed only their shoes. Walt sat in an old, hard-backed chair just inside the door to the room where he could push aside a corner of the window drapery and see any vehicles going either way driving through the motel lot. It was three a.m. The traffic on the highway had dropped down to just an occasional car every ten or fifteen minutes. He was finding it difficult to stay awake. He would occasionally nod off, only to lift his head back up and shake it two or three times. Twice he got up and went into the bathroom to splash cold water on his face. Around four thirty in the morning, he was still fighting sleep. It was time to wake Jim up to take over the watch. Just as he started to get up from his chair, he noticed headlights flash across the room window from a car as it turned off the highway and into the motel parking lot. Walt watched as the vehicle turned toward their end of the motel. It moved slowly through the lot. Occasionally a smaller light would appear shining out of the window of the car. Walt cautiously lifted a small corner of the drapery and peered out into the dark lot. He could clearly make out a County Sheriff's vehicle with a single officer inside. He was driving behind each car in the motel parking lot and shining a flashlight at the plates. It didn't take Walt long to determine which plate he was looking for.

"Jim, wake up," Walt whispered as he tried to rouse him. "Jim, we got company. Deputy Sheriff's car checking out plates. It's just a matter of time 'til he finds the truck."

Jim woke slowly and tried to get his bearings. "What did you say, Walt?"

"Cop in the parking lot checking out cars. We're gonna get made. We need to do something quick."

"Let me slip my shoes on."

Jim tucked in his shirttail and put on his shoes. He grabbed his ball cap and light jacket. As he grabbed a rifle, he said to Walt, " I'm awake now. I'll handle this guy. Get Donald up and ready to go. He can sleep some more in the car. We've got to get going."

"Be careful, Jim. You know they think we're some sort of domestic terrorists. They'll shoot us on sight and ask questions later."

"I got this. Just get the President ready to roll."

Jim killed the small bathroom light and walked over to the door. It was completely dark in the room so no one would notice the door had opened as he slipped out. He dropped to his knees in front of a car that the deputy had just passed. He watched as he drove slowly through the lot to the next car, the last one before the end of the building. When he turned to leave the lot there was no way he wouldn't see the taillights of their truck. As the flashlight beam cleared the last plate, the vehicle began to make its turn. As Jim watched and waited, it came to a sudden halt. The door opened and the deputy stepped out. In a very practiced stealth mode, Jim moved up behind him. He had a flashback to his days in combat as he crept up on the officer, making less sound than the breeze rattling the surrounding trees. With perfect precision, he stood up behind the officer. Just as he started to turn and go back to his vehicle, Jim planted the butt of his rifle squarely onto the back of his head. With just a slight groan, he fell to the ground. Jim reached down and felt the back of his head where a sizable lump was already taking shape. Walt and Donald came up from behind him.

"Is he dead?"

"No, but he'll have a hell of a headache tomorrow. Maybe a concussion, but he'll survive. Help me get him into the truck. Mr. President, would you mind looking into the toolbox behind the cab and get me a roll of duct tape? There are several rolls in there. I never leave home without it."

Together they pushed the officer into the passenger seat of the truck. Jim got in on the driver's side. In less than five minutes, he had the police officer completely bound and gagged with the duct tape.

"OK, Walt. You and Donald drive the police car behind me. Stay tight behind me so nobody can get between us and read my plate. I'm going to find a logging road. We'll drive down it about a half-mile and park the truck. I'll throw the keys away, so he'll have to walk back here if he breaks free. I think he'll be out for at least four or five hours. When he doesn't answer a radio call or show up at the end of his shift, they'll know something's wrong. He'll be fine. We need to cover a lot of miles before this car becomes a moving target for every police officer in the country. Follow me."

Eight miles down the highway, Grimshaw made a left turn onto a gravel road that led to a fire tower. He drove through the think forest for about a half-mile before he pulled over to the side and got out. He planned to drop the keys later as they made their way down the highway. No one would be starting his truck any time soon without a locksmith. He jumped into the back seat of the police car, and the three men took off northbound on I-95 for Washington, D.C. Walt asked the question that had crossed all of their minds the minute they got in a police car.

"Do you think we should cut on the blue lights and just speed like hell?"

Jim replied, "I wondered about that too. I'm not sure it wouldn't draw some attention from other cops along the interstate. We need to run up 95 if we're going to make any kind of time. An out-of-state cop car with the lights on might get us some looks we don't need."

"I guess you're right. It sure is tempting though."

Donald had a question of his own. "This car and the deputy are bound to be missed in the next couple of hours if they haven't figured out already that there's a problem. If they try to reach him on the radio and don't get an answer, they'll be looking for him everywhere in that area. Or if he comes to and manages to flag somebody down, it's not going to be very long before they'll be after us. More than two hours and I think we're pushing our luck in this vehicle."

"I agree. We need to get into another vehicle quickly."

"We can rule out taking one at a convenience store or gas station. There'd be a stolen car report blasted out within a few minutes. We can't get a rental car without identification. You can be sure there's already an all-points bulletin out for the three of us so even a cabbie isn't going to haul somebody three hundred miles without being suspicious. Thumbing isn't a good idea either. Have you got any other thoughts?"

Jim had been thinking about their dilemma for quite some time. "I know exactly what we can do. We go to the same place where we came from."

"Back to Columbus?"

"No. The VFW. We go straight to the next VFW where we can find some folks more like us. We need some real Americans we can trust. We all know that's the best place in the world to look."

"Brilliant. Where do you think we can find one?"

"Any decent-sized city would have one. I know a couple of guys in Savannah. I'm going to point our front bumper in that direction. If you guys want to catch a catnap, go ahead. I'm wide awake. If anything happens, I'll let you know."

Donald and Jim both pushed their heads back into their seats and within seconds the car rattled to the snores of both men. About an hour later, they were awakened when the car left the smooth highway and pulled into the parking lot of a VFW post just outside of Savannah on US 17.

Walt announced, "We're here. It's a little after eight. We made great time. It's nice to not have to drive the speed limit. I want to get some police decals for my truck."

The three men scanned the parking lot to see if anyone could possibly be there that early. Donald sighed as he reported the obvious. "Empty. I guess it's too early for somebody to be here."

"Not too many guys need a beer for breakfast. I've done it in the past, but most of the guys won't show up 'til around lunchtime."

As they were talking, an old Ford F150 pickup pulled in alongside of them. The driver looked to be about seventy years old wearing a beat-up ball cap and a scraggly beard. He pulled in, lining his window up with theirs.

"Are you guys plainclothes or what?"

"Nope. We're doing a little undercover work though. Name's Jim Grimshaw. I'm from the VFW in Columbus."

"Well, it all makes sense now. I know exactly who you fellas are. You're the most wanted men in Georgia, maybe the whole damned country. It's all over the news. I spoke to some of the fellas over at your post and they said not to believe the news. Said you were on the right side of things. I'm Bud Phillips. So, what are you fellas doing here other than hiding out in a stolen cop car?"

"We have a guest with us. Someone you might recognize."

Donald leaned out the window and extended his hand. The look of surprise on the old man's face was unmistakable.

"Well, I'll be. You're Donald Trump, the President."

"Nice to meet you, Bud."

"We thought you were dead. Some of the stations said you weren't. Then the folks at the Pentagon said that was wrong, that you and the First Lady got killed on Air Force One. I'm glad to see you survived. And the First Lady?"

"She's alive and well and in hiding for now. We need your help, Bud."

"You name it. Done my part with the 1st Cav in the Ia Drang Valley. I shoulda been dead forty years ago. I figure I'll never see any action that compares to that. What can I do?"

Jim answered, "This car's got to be hot by now. We need to ditch it and get a ride to D.C. I don't think your truck is big enough. Can you get a car?"

"I can handle that in less than ten minutes with one phone call. Let's get the President into the hall. I'll put some coffee on while you're waiting and I promise you there'll be two or three fellows here in just a few minutes that was coming to help me mow the grass. These are some guys you can count on, Mr. President. All three vets just like me. We're all heartsick about what's happened to our country. We voted for you 'cause we wanted to get those bastards out of there. I guess they didn't like you too much."

"You're right there, Bud. Now, how about that coffee?"

"Follow me inside."

Bud pulled at the hefty key ring hanging from his belt loop and opened the hall up. He put on a pot of coffee while they all pulled up stools alongside the bar. They had secured another ride, but a plan of what to do once they got to the capital was still not clear. They realized that as much pressure as they were under in Georgia from the authorities, it would increase one thousand fold in D.C. They were heading directly into the lion's den. Bud brought over the coffee pot and poured everyone a steaming hot cupful. Bud was a fan of Donald's.

"I was pulling for you from the start. I'd lost all confidence in Washington to have any integrity whatsoever. All of my buddies here at the post felt just the same. Washington is crooked as hell, and the folks running things must be insane. They had a woman running against you that lied every time she opened her mouth. She mishandled top secret information that killed Americans and put many others at risk. She had scandals a mile long in her wake and even dishonored our fellow veterans who had just given their lives for their country by lying to their grieving families. What a witch! And then, your own party went after you like you was on the other side. Hell, if they had gone after Obama half as hard as they did you, he wouldn't have been elected. Most shameless exhibition of corruption we'd ever seen in this country. Now since none of us fell for their shenanigans, they try and get rid of you and your entire family. How are your kids? Are they safe?"

"I'm not certain. They reported there were five people killed in Columbus and there were only three men there protecting them so I can only hope they survived at this point."

"We'll be praying for you, Mr. President."

"Thank you, Bud."

The door to the hall opened and two older veterans came into the room. They walked over to where everyone else was sitting. on bar stools. It hit them as they were saying good morning to everyone just who was sitting there.

"My God, it's President Trump! Mr. President, we thought you were dead."

"As you can see, I'm still very much alive."

"Thank, God. And who are you fellas?"

"I'm Jim Grimshaw and this here's Walt, Walter Edge. We're both from the VFW over in Columbus. We're trying to help the

President get back to the capital and put the heat on the dogs who have taken over up there. I'm sorry to say, but some of the bad ones running the show are within the Pentagon. The worst is General Morrison. Donald, I mean President Trump, says he's one of the ringleaders of this silent coup. We need a bunch of us to help him take back the country."

"That'll be a hell of a lot easier said than done, Jim."

"We know what we're up against. Just like Bud here, this is our Ia Drang Valley. Everywhere we look is the enemy. We've got to stand up against the odds and do whatever it takes to win. I've got about twenty fellas back in Columbus who are in. I trust them with my life. If you all want to help, we can sure use you."

Bud immediately spoke up. "I can't speak for anybody else, but I'm with you."

The other two men affirmed the same.

"I guarantee you I can come up with another twenty guys right here. You just let us know what you want us to do."

"I knew you would feel that way. The first thing need is to get back on the road. I'll give you some phone numbers for my guys back in Columbus. Tell 'em to get everyone together and start heading this way. We'll figure out what to do next while we're on the way. The longer we're on the run, the worse our odds will be. I'll get back up with you when we have some sort of plan. Meanwhile, find your men and make certain there's none among them that you have even the slightest concern that they might not keep quiet about this. If anyone talks, we're all dead."

"I understand. If you fellas have had enough coffee, let's find a car and get on the road. Either of you guys got a car you can lend to me and the President?"

Both men reached in their pockets and produced car keys.

Bud grabbed a set from the man seated closest to him.

"We'll take the big SUV. It's the one with the most room. I got a credit card for gas and food. Anything else we need, Jim?"

"I think we're good. Let's get going."

The four men shook hands with the remaining two and headed for the car.

* * *

General Morrison sat in a room with the leader of the conspirators. There was just the two of them in the room. The general sat rigidly upright in the chair and listened intently. He was sweating and showing a rare sign of nerves that seldom betrayed his countenance.

"So, General. You said this was all over. You said it was taken care of. You told me that our man, Snowden, was going to be sworn in by now. Yet, I see on news channels all over the country that Donald Trump is very much alive. Not only that, he's heading back here to take his rightful place on the throne."

Bitter sarcasm dripped off the man's tongue as he spoke.

"And now, here we are. Many years of hard work, dangerous work that we undertook to stabilize the world, is set to go down the drain because of your incompetence and a renegade politician, a man not fit to hold the office. He's a man we went out of the way to discredit, but the incredibly stupid public thought they knew best. In spite of all the evidence we put out on him clearly depicting him as dangerous, a con artist, a fraud, and they still put this moron in the White House. And you. You guaranteed me that he and his wife would have a glorious ending in the Middle East. Again, a failure. Then you said he would be eliminated as a threat when he reached Georgia. And here we sit. Waiting for his arrival in Washington. I guess we should stand in front of the Lincoln

Memorial or on the lawn at the Mall and greet the conquering warrior as he strides back to his kingdom on a white horse. I'm not going to do that. I'm not even giving that a moment's thought. Here's what's going to happen. For your sake, it better happen. You and our people will be watching everywhere in this city. Airports, subways, train stations, bus stations, tollbooths and even public restrooms will all be under 24/7 surveillance. All day, all night, no one sleeps; no one even blinks until we find Donald Trump. I don't want him brought to me. I don't want his arrival noticed by anyone. I don't want to hear that something unfortunate happened to him. What I want is to never hear from him again. He will never show up here and I'll never have to deal with him, through you, ever again. How clear can I make this to you?"

"I understand completely, sir. We are on highest alert. When he turns up, we'll be there."

"Please, stop. Don't even tell me about all the great things you're going to do. I don't want to hear anything more from you other than you calling me and saying, 'it's over.' Are we on the same page? Have I made myself perfectly clear?"

"We are, sir. You have, sir"

"Get out of here and make it happen."

"Yes, sir."

13

It was late in the afternoon and the commuters leaving the capital had created the daily traffic nightmare that is Washington, D.C. Those leaving the city well outnumbered those coming in. Jim, Walt, Donald and Bud were tired but their adrenalin levels had been elevated for hours so it overcame their exhaustion. The drive to D.C. had been slow. They had realized they couldn't go through any tollbooths on the approach to the city. Every time one lay ahead, they had to exit the highway and look for an alternate route. As soon as they could, they'd re-enter the highway and the process would start all over. It was tiring but necessary. Now that traffic was all around them, Donald had to keep his face completely out of anyone's line of sight. He borrowed Bud's ball cap, his light jacket and turned the collar up while sitting low in the seat. He was anxious for darkness to settle in so he could quit worrying about being spotted. By 8:30 p.m., they were in Tyson's Corner, Virginia, parked just outside of the VFW hall. It was dark, and there were only a few cars at the post. Jim offered to go in first.

"They're bound to have gotten notice to be on the lookout for us. I'll go in first by myself and assess the situation."

"Be careful. We've come a long way to wind up in trouble so close to our destination."

"Count on it."

Jim walked in and took a quick look around. The place was almost empty. There were two guys at a table and the hall manager was cleaning up. He walked over to the table and spoke with the men seated there.

"Mind if I join you?"

"Please do. Want a beer?"

"That would be great, but in a minute. I've got a couple of questions I need help with."

"Let's hear 'em."

"First, I'm Jim Grimshaw, a retired Ranger from Columbus, Georgia. Spent twenty-three years mostly under fire. At the moment, I'm on the most dangerous mission of my life."

"Where are the cameras? This sounds like some sort of TV reality show or something. What's the bottom line?"

"When I tell you, it's going to sound even more unbelievable. President Trump is in the car outside. We're on the run from a group that has seized power at the Pentagon and a number of other agencies in D.C."

One of the men responded immediately.

"I saw a news report the other night. It had President Trump with some kind of headline from a newspaper to prove he didn't die when Air Force One was blown up. Is that what this is all about? You really have him with you? No shit?"

"I do and we need your help big time. We've been leaning on VFW members for the past couple of days to help us get him back to D.C. He's going to try to throw a wrench at these conspirators and we're going help him do whatever we can to get it done. You guys are of my generation and I know you can't be happy about how things are going up here."

"Amen to that, brother. No doubt about it. I'll do what I can to help President Trump. I voted for him just like everybody I know who's sick of the lying thieves up here. The clowns running the V.A. shoulda all been in prison ten years ago. Why don't you bring him on in here? It's getting cold outside."

"All right, but we have to count on absolute confidence in what we do. Anybody talks to the wrong people, and this will all explode in our faces. I'll be right back."

Thirty seconds later, both of the men waiting inside were incredulous as the President entered the room. They recognized him instantly rising to greet him as he came over to them.

"Gentlemen, thank you for offering to help me. I'm Donald Trump."

"Yes, sir, Mr. President. I sure know who you are. I'd know your face anywhere. Please, sit down. Can I get you a beer? How 'bout some coffee? You name it."

"To tell you the truth, I think a coffee would be just right."

"I'll get you a hot cup right now. By the way, I'm Randy. Randy Moore. Retired Gunnery Sergeant. USMC. And that other old guy there is my buddy, Elgin."

Elgin Taylor stood up and shook Donald's hand.

"It's an honor, sir."

"No, it's my privilege to have met so many true patriots these last couple of days. I trust all of the veterans I've met more than I do the people who are running the entire military today. You all have been what made America great. Those D.C. weasels are what is killing her. We have to eradicate the cancer that's taken hold in Washington."

"We're with you on that, sir."

The old gunnery sergeant brought back several frosted mugs and a pitcher of beer. He passed out the mugs and then poured a cup of coffee for Donald. He set the pitcher in the middle of the table and everyone poured their own. He joined them at the small table.

"So, can one of you fill us in on what in the hell this is all about and what you intend to do about it?"

Jim took a deep swallow of the ice-cold beer and smiled as he let it slowly trickle down the back of his throat.

"Damn that's good. Just what I needed. I'll bring you up to speed on what's been going on."

After an hour or so, everyone in the room understood all of the facts right up to the moment. However, they still had no word on his kids and there was still no roadmap going forward as to how best to get Donald Trump back in charge of the capital. Donald poured himself another half cup of coffee.

"On the surface, this is kind of like a pee wee football team taking on the Green Bay Packers. It just doesn't seem like something we can do. One thing we can all agree on though is that whatever we decide here tonight is going to be dangerous. The people we're dealing with are completely ruthless and devoid of any appreciation or attachment to the country. They have some sort of worldview where there's a central government in control of virtually everything, and of course, they run it. They know I'm alive and that I'll be trying to upset their plans. In this entire area, they have cameras and ears everywhere. I don't really know who they've corrupted in any agency. The best chance I have is you guys. Veterans from a bygone era with traditional values and a sense of duty to their country. It gives me great hope to have met you all. Do any of you have some ideas on what we can do?"

Jim had been thinking on that subject for two days. He was beginning to develop a strategy.

"It's obvious we can't take on the U.S. government, nor the military, nor the police. They're all way too large. No, we need to go at them from the inside. One thing that's certain about every type of government organization up in D.C. is the fact that there are a lot of retired military working for them. If we can pick out a few in strategic positions that will help us, we can cause a lot of havoc. I know that some of the guys who served with me are working up here now. I guarantee you none of them are involved in any type of anti-American conspiracy. They'd die first. Is there a list somewhere of the VFW members who are still working up here?"

Randy walked over to the desk by the kitchen door.

"This is what you're talking about right here. It's a list of all our members. I know all of them. You'll see name, address and a phone number for every one of them. It's a good group of guys."

"Here's what I'd like to know. Do any of them work for the Capitol Police?"

"Our friend Butch Watson works for the Capitol Police. He's retired Army. He was in a bomb disposal unit for years. Now he's one of the big shots for the Capitol Police Bomb Squad. He's a straight-up guy. He'd help the President any way he could. I guarantee you he would."

Jim's mind was spinning.

"Now that has real potential. Donald, when do you want to make your move against Morrison?"

"Today is Tuesday, right?"

"That's right."

"I'd like to set up some sort of public meeting, as soon as possible. The longer we wait the more time they have to prepare. We need to have the press and a lot cameras there as I come back to the capital. Sort of a grand entrance you might say. Just the fact that I'm still alive will bring out every type of media in the country. These rogues won't do anything aggressive toward me in front of that many cameras. Granted they control some of the heavy hitters in the big networks, but we'll make sure every little independent station we can get hold of is there. We'll literally call them and I'll tell them to be there. I think we need to set this up for tomorrow evening. Can you pull things together by then?"

"I think so. Randy, I need to meet this guy Butch in the morning, first thing. Can you make that happen?"

"I'll have him here by eight tomorrow morning. What else?"

"I think we're going to need about twenty to thirty vets at our side. Any more than that would be counter-productive. I'm afraid that if we get too many people involved, the word might get back to Morrison as to what we have planned. I'm not a dreamer. We have to face the fact that what we're doing is risky. Truth is, the odds are stacked heavily against us. Let's get on the horn tonight and pick the best guys we can get. I know there's some who would want to help, but are just too old and infirmed. Don't even mention it to them. Get the best of the best. Let's have everybody here tomorrow afternoon around four. Put out the word that the lodge had a sewage problem and will be closed for two days. Walt, you help the President contact the media folks he wants to alert and decide where to hold this little gathering. I'm beginning to get a picture in my mind of how to make this happen. I'll know more in the morning. Now, how about a little more beer? If we only have a couple more days on the planet, I'm gonna want to have a few more cold beers before I check out."

The six men passed around a couple more pitchers of beer and the conversation grew a little more nostalgic for the older veterans. Being a teetotaler, Donald nevertheless enjoyed the comradery with these old-school soldiers. After perhaps just one beer too many, Bud began to talk about a terrifying night on the knoll at Ia Drang Valley.

"I was young and I was tough as hell. At least I thought I was. I'd been through all the training, didn't have no problems with any of it. I liked it. The harder it was, the more it suited me. I was anxious to see combat. I was like a well-trained boxer waiting to get in the ring for his fight. I was champing at the bit. They set us down in a grassy field. We started taking sniper fire right away. Two boys in my company bought the farm in the first ten minutes. It's a sobering thing to watch somebody's life just go away in an instant. One minute, you're talking with them, and the next they're gone forever. Their body is just lying there on the ground with nothing behind their eyes. It's scary to see. They were so young. Several other guys got hit and the moaning started. It kept up for almost two days. There was somebody being killed or wounded every couple of minutes. At first, I couldn't even see the guys that were shooting at us. They were hiding in the jungle behind thick underbrush. Occasionally you'd see a tracer. You'd hear the constant popping sounds. I thought to myself, well, we're the U.S. Army. It won't be long and we'll have this under control. We get too much fire coming at us and we'll have some jets come overhead and fill their pants up with napalm. It didn't work out that way. More and more of them came at us. It was like there was an unending line of them. It didn't matter how many we killed, they just kept coming. My squad got orders to set up a fire line on the knoll where we could have a good view of anybody coming up at us. We moved over and we saw plenty of them coming. It was becoming real clear that we were heavily outnumbered. We called for backup and it never came. We were alone all night up on the knoll. At first, we'd see them coming from the tree line in front of us and they were pretty far away. It was like shooting at shadows. They'd move toward us and we'd pop 'em. They were falling fast, but it never slowed 'em down. I kept asking myself, how many of them are there? They just kept coming. It'd slow down for a little while, and then they'd regroup and start all over. Before dark even set in, half of my squad was dead or wounded. There was just a few of us left that could put up any kind of a fight, and I knew they'd keep coming through the night. It's one thing to shoot at shadows thirty yards away, but later they got so close I could look 'em right in their eyes as they came at us. They were young too, and you could see they was just as scared as we were. That didn't really help to know. They were firing at us, and we were firing at them. It went on for what seemed like days. It was one night, just one. I never slept. I killed so many I lost count. Twice they broke through our fire line, and we had to fight them on the ground. I killed three with my pistol and one with my knife. I watched him, his face six inches from mine and I swear I could see his soul leave his body. He couldn't have been over twenty. I'll never forget his face. I don't know why I'm still alive. Shouldn't be. Shoulda died that night on the knoll, like most of my buddies did. I've wondered about that ever since. You know, maybe this is why I'm still here. Tonight, I'm here to help my President save the country. That would explain it, wouldn't it?"

Donald patted him on the back. "It sure would, Bud. It sure would."

Bud leaned back, wiped a single tear from his wrinkled cheek and took a deep swallow of draft beer.

Jim opened up a little on his history. "I wasn't there, Bud. I had some friends who were. A couple didn't make it. With the number of bullets I dodged during my time with Uncle Sam, I don't think I missed much. Five wars on three continents and the worst times I had were in places where we supposedly weren't even at war. Those are always fun. You die there, and nobody ever finds out what really happened to you. Your wife gets a sad note from the Army saying you died in an unfortunate training accident. I love those. Five wars, two Purple Hearts and I promise you the folks who signed my checks never even heard of me. And after defending my country for decades, here I am trying to help the President take it back from a bunch of worthless bastards who have tried to steal it. I want to get after them even worse than those terrorists in the Middle East. I'm going to give this all I got."

"I have to tell you, Jim. Not everyone in the Middle East is living two thousand years behind the rest of the world. If it weren't for several Arab friends getting Melania and me out of Yemen, I'd be in the ground right now. There are many fanatics over there. I'll grant you that. But just like everywhere else in the world, there're good people and there're bad. We've got the bad after us right here at home as we speak."

Jim nodded as he listened. He would be hard to convince there was much good in an area of the world where he had been the target of so much violence. He looked at his friends and then back at Donald as he said, "Well, I need a little shuteye. I'm going to collapse right here on the carpeted section of floor. I'll see you fellas in a few hours. In just minutes, the room was dark and quiet.

* * *

Just after the first few rays of sun appeared through cracks in the old venetian blinds, the place smelled of fresh coffee. The six men who'd spent the night in the VFW hall were rousing themselves from a hard night's sleep.

Donald remarked out loud, "I think I've set a record here. Four days without changing my socks. Before we set up my homecoming, I'm going to have to wash and press these clothes at the least."

Randy volunteered, "I've got you covered there, Mr. President. My wife is an ironing machine. I'll run them to the house and stay there while she does 'em. Meanwhile, you can slip on a pair of coveralls we got in the storage room. We use them to work on the place. I'll get you a pair."

Grimshaw had only one thought on his mind. "Hey, Randy. Did you get up with the guy from the bomb squad?"

"Affirmative. He'll be here within the hour."

"Does he know what we're doing here?"

"Nope. But when he hears what's going on, you won't be able to hold him back from helping. He's what the media calls a radical rightwing activist. His favorite expression is 'my country, right or wrong.' He'll jump at the chance to help."

"That sounds great. Walt, you gonna help Donald set up this little get-together with the media and General Morrison?"

"Yeah, but I still don't understand what's going to keep him from just grabbing us all the minute we show up and then announcing the meeting's been called off. I mean, the last thing he wants to do is let Donald speak freely to the press. He'll see us all dead first. Don't forget the boys back in Georgia. He practically had an army after them. He's got a lot of resources at his beck and call. And worse than that, we don't even know who's playing ball with him."

Grimshaw answered the statement, as he knew it created doubt in everyone's mind. "Just set it all up the way the President wants and I'll personally take care of the general. I'll tell you all about it this afternoon. Let me see if I can make it work first. If I can't, then we'll go back to plan B."

"What is Plan B?"

"Hide out in the mountains."

" I'm good with that. I like the mountains."

A loud knock on the door to the lodge startled everyone inside.

Randy spoke up, "That'll be Butch. I'll let him in."

He opened the door and Butch Watson walked in like he owned the place. He was six foot three and over two hundred fifty pounds of muscle. Even in his late sixties, he was still as fit as a twenty-year old. His presence was larger than life, like John Wayne. Randy made the introductions. Jim shook his hand and motioned him over to a table.

"Randy tells me you're running things for the Capitol Police Bomb Disposal Unit."

"That would be me. What's so important I have to take off from work this morning to come visit with you guys?"

"I've got a story to tell you, Butch. You might find it somewhat hard to grasp. Before I do, let me introduce you to someone. It might lend some credibility to what I'm going to tell you. Come with me."

They walked over to the other side of the room where Walt and Donald were making notes about tomorrow's events. Donald was without a shirt and wearing only the long bib overalls that Randy had given him. He had his back toward Grimshaw and Butch.

"Donald, let me introduce you to someone."

Donald turned around and stuck out his hand. "I'm Donald Trump."

Butch was incredulous. "You're, you're the President. I thought you were killed a few days ago."

"Well, as you can see, I'm still among the living. Thanks to a little luck and the men around us here."

"It's a privilege to meet you, sir. What are you doing here? What can I do to help you? Where are your clothes?"

"I'll let Jim go into that with you. But, Butch..."

"Yes, sir?"

"It's good to have you aboard."

"Yes, sir. You can count on me."

Jim and Butch spent the next two hours huddled deep in conversation. By midday, Jim had engineered what he thought was a workable plan with a reasonable chance of success. He sat down at the table with Walt and Donald.

"Mr. President, I guess we're about there. Did you get up with the television stations and newspapers you were wanting to call?"

"Yes. I'm not sure how many will actually show up. A lot of them were very skeptical of what I was telling them. Of course, it is pretty unbelievable. Walter got us the building."

Walt beamed as he spoke, "I've known the district manager over there for twenty years. I told him we've got a media event planned and we wanted to announce it over there. He says he'll keep it quiet. He's gonna be pretty surprised when everybody starts showing up over there tomorrow. It's the district VFW hall over on Maryland Avenue. It's a big place with a large meeting room that will work perfectly. Not a lot of doors to monitor. Twenty-seven guys will be here later today. Their ages average in the late sixties, but they're people who still have fight in them and that you can count on. How did things go with Butch?"

"We're all set. By late night we'll either be a free country again or our little group here will have matching orange jump suits. What's left to do?"

"I want to call General Morrison, but I'll wait until about six p.m. I want to make it as difficult as possible on him to figure out how to deal with us. I'll give him the least amount of time possible. I'm willing to bet we've already fired up his ulcer this week. If anybody ever deserved it, it's him."

❋ ❋ ❋

General Morrison was in his office deep within the Pentagon along with the other members of the Joint Chiefs. It didn't take long to see the concern on all of their faces. Morrison tried to remain positive and in command as he spoke to them.

"We are in the driver's seat here. I don't think we have a thing to worry about. As soon as Trump contacts us, we'll start the ball rolling. I know he'll want any meeting with us to be in a public place and with a lot of media there. He knows we control the big networks, so he'll undoubtedly have a bunch of local affiliates there, especially that pathetic little station in Kansas City who broke the story for him. As soon as this affair is done, their FCC license is going to be pulled. You can bank on that. The moment we find out the location, we'll have our people and the Secret Service cover the place like a blanket. He'll be leaving with us. His little speech will never happen. I'm afraid that all of the stress in the crash of Air Force One, the loss of so many friends in the fiery crash and the unfortunate loss of his children has pushed President

Trump to the limit and he suffered a massive heart attack. We'll break the sad news to the media two hours later, swear in Snowden, and plan a magnificent state funeral. It's going to be beautiful. Full military honors, of course."

One of the generals spoke up. "You make this all sound pretty simple. There have already been too many failures in this whole affair. If you don't finish the job this time, I'm afraid we'll be pushing our luck. It's not possible to cover every base every time. Make this time the last time."

"I'm taking no chances. As soon as I get the location, we'll start final preparations. No stone unturned. Thank you, gentlemen. I'll see you all this evening."

He spoke with bearing and confidence, but inside his heart rate had escalated considerably. There had been one disaster after another and it couldn't continue. The people he answered to would not accept anything less than an absolute end to this nightmare.

14

Donald understood more than anyone how much was on the line. It wasn't just his presidency or democracy; it was everyone's future. It was potentially the end of a free society. The men who had gathered around him were prepared to give their lives if that's what was required of them, and so was he. The odds against them were staggering. He and a few dozen grizzled old veterans were going to try to overthrow a collection of traitors and the massive military might that they controlled. On the surface, it appeared to be completely impossible but they were the only chance left for the country. This would be the day that either the world was saved by American patriots or it would fall into an evil darkness controlled by tyrants. Donald walked over to Jim Grimshaw as he was drinking his second cup of coffee and getting ready to meet with a ragtag collection of twenty-six men. They all clearly understood the danger. Most of them had laid their lives on the line before and weren't about to back down at this critical time. To look at the aging, pot-bellied, bearded group, one would never guess the cumulative combat experience that was standing there. These were serious people with a single mindset, the desire to save what they all believed in. Many more would have happily stepped up, but Jim determined that those who were handpicked were the best choice possible to attempt the dramatic move being planned.

Donald pulled Jim to the side. "All right, Jim. Are we ready to go? How do you feel about our chances?"

"I'm hopeful, Mr. President. We don't have a lot of resources to pull from. These are some great warriors gathered here with us. The truth is, I don't think anyone would give us much of a chance, but look at what happened with Robin Hood and Little John. Sometimes the good guys can pull it off. We can't go at these people with a frontal attack. We wouldn't last two minutes. What we're going to do can best be described as sleight of hand. We're setting up an illusion of sorts."

"That's encouraging, Jim, but I'm pretty sure Robin Hood was fiction."

"It's the best I could come up with on short notice."

Jim chuckled at his own joke as he took another swig of coffee. Donald actually felt a little relieved to see that Jim could be so relaxed and under control during such a stressful time.

"They know it's a big moment, so they'll be there. The one detail we left out was to tell them where this gathering would be held. If we had told them earlier, it's certain Morrison would have found out from one of them and had a lot more time to prepare the place and set up his trap. There are maybe a dozen stations waiting for our call. They understand it will be in the capital, so they're close by. At two hours out, we'll call every one of them and give them the location. They'll be there."

"And Morrison will be getting a call when we're ready for him to know where it's going to be held. We need to be certain we're ready before we give him the location. I'm sure he's expecting it. He has just as much to worry about as we do. There's going to be quite a few unexpected moments in today's events. I just hope they all go our way."

"They have to. The country is counting on us. They just don't know it."

A harried Butch Watson entered the room. He walked over to Grimshaw and pulled him aside. "Jim, I'm concerned."

"What's up?"

"When I started putting my crew together, I went to only the guys I knew would be a hundred percent reliable and could keep their mouths shut. I know it wasn't any of them who spilled the beans."

"Spilled them about what?"

"What we're doing here."

"How do you know somebody said something?"

"When I spoke to one of my oldest buddies he already knew something was up. He said the word was out from some of the vets in the other halls up and down the coast. I don't think any of them would have gone to Morrison knowing what was about to happen but some of them have been talking and I don't know how far the talk has gotten out. Should we pull the plug on the operation?"

"It's too late. Everything's set. If we stop now, the advantage will transfer back to Morrison. They don't know where it's going to be or what our plans are, as far as we know. We're going to have to trust that no one has blown our cover and follow the plan we've come up with. I'm not saying anything to anybody, not even Donald. He's got enough to worry about without this news. Just have faith, my friend. We've been in tighter spots than this before."

"OK, Jim. It's your call and I'm with you."

At four p.m. Donald was handed a WiFi-powered telephone. The VFW hall would be empty before any of Morrison's staff could begin to track down the location of the call. He pushed the send button for Morrison's private line at the Pentagon.

"General Morrison's office. May I help you?"

"Yes, tell General Morrison it's the President calling."

"Yes, sir, Mr. President. He's been expecting your call."

"I'm sure he has."

"This is General Morrison."

"Enjoy the moment, Morrison. Soon, no one will be saying 'general' before your name."

"Time will tell, Donald. What is this earth-shaking message you have for me?"

Morrison looked over at Lieutenant Drexler and made a circular motion with his hand to let him know the monitoring and tracking systems needed to be in high gear. Drexler nodded and gave a thumbs up back at him to let him know it began with the first ring of the phone.

"We're having a press briefing this evening with a few select stations that don't stick to your spoon-fed propaganda. It's called the free press. I thought you might want to be there to hear what I have to say to them."

"I certainly do. Just tell me the where and when and I will see you there."

"It will be at Ketchum Hall. Certainly you're familiar with that location."

"The VFW hall on Maryland Avenue. I've spoken there many times. A great location. And when will this affair take place?"

"Six p.m. That's a little under two hours from now. You really need to take time out from your long day of plotting against your own country and try to attend."

"Oh, I'll be there. You can count on it."

"Great, Morrison. I'll see you there."

Within thirty seconds General Morrison had gathered his key aides and set about planning how to prevent Donald from speaking to anyone.

"Our informant at the station was correct. It's not far from here. We now know the time and place. You all know where the VFW hall is on Maryland Avenue. Let's get over there and be ready for him when he shows up. Also, Lieutenant Drexler, you remember the things we talked about yesterday? Make them happen."

"Yes, sir."

In short order, a large military presence began forming around the old VFW hall. Guards were posted on every corner. Secret Service agents took positions inside the building and at every entrance. Even the nearby rooftops had Morrison's people stationed on them. They would see Donald Trump long before he got anywhere close to the building. Secret Service secured their positions. Camera crews and reporters from the media outlets began to appear. They were startled by the large military contingent there. Some reporters began to broadcast as soon as they arrived and could set up a camera. With just an hour to go before Donald was supposed to be speaking, the entire area had become a media circus. Capitol Police were called in to close off streets and stop curiosity-seeking pedestrian traffic. Officers patrolling with K-9 units were stationed at every corner. No one there understood the ramifications of what they were witnessing and none was prepared for what would actually occur. Into the center of the commotion, General Morrison pulled up in a staff car, followed by several cars containing Secret Service personnel. As he exited the car, he looked around at the extensive army of media and the growing crowd of onlookers gathered along the street in every direction.

"Good Lord, how did so many people get here this quickly? It's going to be difficult to get this crowd under control. Drexler, I want some organization put into this street situation out here. I don't want anyone coming between us and Trump. He's using the crowd to mask what he's got planned. Be careful what's being filmed. We're not here to do a documentary, understand?"

"Yes, sir. I'll get some troops in here and stabilize the area immediately."

Morrison was growing concerned about the size of the crowd and what impact it could have on removing Trump before he could begin speaking to the public. What neither he nor even Donald and his cohorts realized was the fact that the crowd was escalating at a huge rate with a disproportionate number of serious-looking old vets filling in every void in the entire area. The whispers Butch had warned Grimshaw about had become a shout and then a very loud roar. Vietnam-era veterans were appearing like seaweed on the beach after a flood tide. Vanloads of veterans were approaching the last roadblocks and emptying their overstuffed compartments onto the streets. Several groups drove up on motorcycles and still others in SUVs and RVs. They positioned themselves adjacent to any military or police presence in the area. Many of them looked like an extracted scene from "Easy Rider" with their antique Army jackets or motorcycle leathers featuring the American flag. It wasn't an Army, but it was a very large gathering of men who were deeply loyal to their country. The thought that someone might be trying to undermine what they had risked their lives for was something they would stand against. They were old, but they were still strong and willing to lay it all on the line one more time. The police manning the street corners and sidewalks were beginning to notice that they were being literally outnumbered by the presence of all these old soldiers. Several messages were conveyed to Morrison's staff about the developing crowds. The general was not alarmed.

"Who did you expect would show up at a VFW hall? Veterans of Foreign Wars, right? Most of these guys are approaching seventy by now. Two-thirds of them are drunks or on heart medicine or some other kind of drugs. Just do what you're told and keep the crowd under control. We'll take care of the rest of it. Just maintain order. Got it?"

The young officer who had brought this situation to his attention snapped a crisp salute to the general.

"Yes, sir!"

"Good. Now let's get back to business."

The general had a temper that didn't react suppress?] well when things were beyond his control. He did his best to hide any outward show of anger, but he was beginning to fume. It didn't help his concern when a reporter and an accompanying cameraman approached him, microphone in hand.

"General Morrison, are you here representing the Joint Chiefs? I have to say it's somewhat surprising to see you here personally. What's the reason you've chosen to be at this gathering with the President?"

"First, I'm not so sure he's actually going to be here. As you know, there were false reports a couple of days ago from some irresponsible media outlets reporting that he was not killed in

Yemen and now this announcement. This could be terrorists manipulating the press. Nobody knows the source of these so-called 'announcements.' The Pentagon has great concern over the safety of this gathering. There's already been a bomb threat called in within the past hour. We believe there is a fanatical group trying to undermine stability here in the capital. I'm here to make sure that doesn't happen. This meeting, if it happens, will be peaceful and no outside extremist group or homegrown terrorist is going to have any impact on how the government does business. I've devoted my life to my country and it's too precious to me to let anything happen to change the way America functions. I have no further comments. It would be advisable for you and your cameraman to stay back a ways from the front entrance to the building. We need to keep that area open in case of any sort of emergency."

"Thank you, General Morrison. That was General Claiborne Morrison speaking just now. He is the current Chairman of the Joint Chiefs. This is Sharon Billings reporting from the capital."

Ketchum Hall was full to the point of overcrowding. The Fire Marshall made a brief appearance. He quickly determined it wouldn't be possible to remove such a large group with television cameras rolling in every direction. Hopefully, it would be over soon and everyone would disperse peacefully on their own. Ketchum Hall was a moderate-sized auditorium. It was now standing room only inside. At every corner of the room, a camera crew was anxiously awaiting whatever would happen. With less than an hour to go before the scheduled appearance of the President, Secret Service were still checking every foot of the entire structure. Two Secret Service agents were tasked to check out the basement located directly under the hall. At the steps leading down to the basement, two uniformed Capitol Police officers were standing guard. One of the Secret Service agents stopped to question them as he reached the first step.

"How long have you been here?"

"We set up a post here about thirty minutes ago. Our bomb crew swept the entire room for explosives. It was clean, so we were posted here to keep everyone out. You're welcome to check it out as well."

"We will. Don't let anyone else down here. Understand?"

"Of course. Just because we don't wear cheap black suits doesn't mean were stupid."

There was a lot of resentment between the regular State Capitol police officers who were tasked with maintaining the safety of the nation's most prized treasures along with its elected officials and the much higher-paid federal agents whose inflated egos pissed them off no end. The two agents began their descent down the steep set of steps leading to the basement.

One of them yelled back to the police, "Any lights down here?"

"Just inside the metal door at the bottom of the stairs. On the right. I know it's pretty complicated."

One of the agents looked at the other. "Capitol Clowns. What a bunch of idiots."

They opened the metal door and looked into the completely dark room. The smell of mold and mildew were thick in the damp air. It smelled like the crawl space of an old house. One of the agents pulled a flashlight from his suit pocket. It produced a small but intense beam of light. He turned it toward the wall where the light switch was supposed to be located. Neither of the agents made the first sound as their limp bodies fell to the concrete basement floor. It was stunning how quickly the two old Rangers eliminated both government agents. They were business-like and extremely efficient at quietly taking out the opposition. Jim and several other men pulled them away from the bottom of the stairs and over to a distant corner of the basement.

After letting one of the dead agent's legs fall to the floor, Jim said, "Two down, dozens to go."

Donald was standing nearby. Surrounded by a dozen armed men, all sworn to go to their final reward protecting him. Jim walked over to the basement door, cracked it open and looked up at the two cops. He gave them thumbs up and they discreetly nodded back to him. He quietly closed the door.

He looked over to Walt. "Walt, did you get the radios off those two?"

"Got them right here."

"Have somebody monitor them. Check the bodies for identification. If anybody calls for either of them on the radio, make sure they get a very garbled answer. We've only got a few minutes left before this all starts to go down."

By this time, the crowds around the VFW hall had swelled to thousands. Two-thirds of them looked remarkably similar. They represented virtually every VFW Lodge on the east coast from Savannah to D.C. On one street corner, an elderly vet turned to his buddy who had made the trip with him on a motorcycle all the way from Florence, South Carolina.

"Who woulda thought this would be the hill we'd die on? Don't matter. The last forty years have been a gift anyway. Shoulda bought the farm in '65 with Vinnie Farina. A good man, I still miss him. I'm doing this for him and my other buddies that didn't make it home. I owe 'em. We all do. Not gonna let some sleazy, bastard traitor step on the flag. Not while I'm alive."

The old soldier turned to the young enlisted soldier stationed a few yards away. "Private. Yes, you. Got a problem over here."

The young soldier moved over toward him. "Yes, sir. What's the problem?"

Within seconds, four old vets surrounded him. One grabbed his rifle and yanked it from his unsuspecting arm. Two others got hold of his arms. In short order they were in control.

"Son, we don't want to hurt you. We're all vets here. General Morrison has led a coup against the President and we're here today to see to it that it don't happen. President Trump is going to be speaking in just a minute in the VFW Hall and we're going to make sure he survives that speech. Are you going to give us any problem? You can have your gun back when the President is done. Are you going to give us any problem?"

The young soldier looked at the four men surrounding him. "No, sir. You don't hurt anybody and I'll just stand here with you."

"Very smart, young man. You'll do fine."

Throughout the area, the same sort of confrontation was occurring again and again. They didn't all go so peacefully. At one of the roadblocks, a contingent of six armed soldiers and two Capitol Police stood guard alongside their armored car. Four old vets approached them riding their chrome-laden Harleys. An officer held up his hand indicating they should stop. They complied and threw down the kickstands on their bikes. A Capitol Police sergeant walked over beside them to tell them they wouldn't be allowed to stay there.

"You can't park your bikes here. You need to get back on them and head about three blocks south to the public parking lot. Then you can walk back over here, if there's room for you, which doesn't really seem likely at this point."

Kevin Marshall walked over to face the officer. He was sixty-eight years old, with a sizeable beer belly and unkempt beard. His face contained lines earned from years in service to the country and for the past twenty as a bricklayer. He was not a man to be trifled with or to mince words.

"I think we're going to leave our bikes right here. You say that's going to be a problem, heh?"

"You heard me right the first time. If you don't leave now, we'll have to arrest you and have your bikes impounded. There's an important event going on down the block and we have to keep these lanes open in case of any problem where an ambulance or police car might be needed. You'll have to move your bikes now."

"That's just not going to happen, officer. We're here to go to the meeting. We understand that the President is speaking and we're big fans of his. So, we'll be leaving our bikes right here and they better be here, untouched when we get back. Have you got that?"

The officer turned to his fellow officers and the accompanying soldiers. "Arrest these men. Have a truck brought in to load their bikes up. Take them to the station and the bikes to the impound yard. They can pay to get them back after the judge releases them. Sorry, gentlemen but you'll have to go with the officers. I warned you."

Kevin didn't flinch. Neither did the dozen or so other old vets who came up from behind the soldiers out of the crowd. With extreme quickness, the vets immediately overpowered the smaller number of soldiers and police. Several men tried to resist and were pummeled to the pavement by the older men who were considerably tougher than they looked. Electrical wire ties were placed on their wrists and their own weapons were used to escort them back to their armored car. After removing the key from the vehicle, the men were herded inside and two of the vets stood watch, one on either side of the car. The remainder of the veterans replaced the soldiers at their watch station by the roadblock. The same process was happening on virtually every street corner. Most ended quietly and were handled in a professional manner by men who understood exactly how to handle such a situation. On four rooftops, vets approached armed snipers from behind and disarmed them within seconds, and would hold them as prisoners until they received word that the President was safe. Two snipers who tried to sound an alert received blows to their heads from the butts of pistols that sent them down to the tar-covered gravel under their feet. Donald Trump, Grimshaw and his men had no knowledge of this additional army of veterans that were providing critical assistance in their mission. In just minutes, those forces were gaining control of the entire area.

General Morrison and a cadre of staff members were gathered backstage waiting for word that the President had been spotted and hopefully apprehended before anyone from the media could spot him. They paced nervously and kept checking their watches.

Drexler noted out loud, "Four minutes 'til six. It should be any moment."

"We'll get him, Drexler. Check all of our stations and see if there's any sign of anything going on."

"Yes, sir."

Drexler said to the senior Secret Service officer, "General Morrison says to do a roll call. Every station."

The agent turned to a subordinate and they began a radio check with each of their men in the building. They had no idea of the turn of events outside. Walt heard the radio go off beside him asking for a report from one of the deceased agents lying on the floor just ten feet away. He took the radio over to an electric panel on the wall of the room. He held the antenna of the small radio to a ground wire inside the old electric box. The radio began to produce a high degree of static as he spoke quietly. "All clear."

The agent listening to the reports could barely make out anything but the vague sound of the all-clear report.

"Browning, you need to check the squelch on your radio. It's got a lot of static."

He moved on to the next station for a report.

Walt looked over at Butch standing beside him. "Oldest trick in the book. Where do they get these guys?"

One block away from the VFW hall, a roadblock had been set up. There were four Capitol Police officers manning the station. Just in front of them, a small traffic jam was starting to form as workers leaving the capital found their customary route blocked. Behind them, a blue flashing light appeared, winding between the cars that were creeping along. Twice it left the roadway and drove onto the right-of-way to get around them. It came up to the roadblock. The officers recognized the vehicle as one of their own. It was an armored vehicle from the bomb squad. The large, enclosed van pulled over to them. The window rolled down and Butch Watson, head of the bomb detail, informed them, "Another bomb threat inside. Let us through now. This has to be quick."

Without hesitation, the officers pulled back the sawhorses and pylons blocking the street and let them pass. Inside the van behind the driver's seat and a steel door, ten vets from Grimshaw's unit were tightly packed. Each of them was wearing a Capitol Police bomb squad uniform. Butch turned his head around slightly so he could say to them, "First hurdle out of the way. We'll be in the parking lot in ten seconds. Get ready. Keep your headgear on and let me do the talking. Remember, we're here to answer a bomb threat."

Earl Dorsett, manager of the VFW hall walked over to General Morrison and the senior Secret Service agent and alerted them, "We've had a bomb threat called in. The Capitol Police Bomb Squad has just arrived. We had the building swept an hour ago. It's probably a stupid prank, but we've got to do another quick sweep of the place. The head of the bomb squad is with them. It shouldn't take long."

The large double metal doors at the back of the building opened and the Capitol Police Bomb Disposal Unit entered the building. They had on their protective gear and every member of the unit seemed to know exactly what needed to be done. It was a drill they had rehearsed many times before. Butch Watson went over to Earl as he stood by General Morrison.

"We're not going to evacuate the building. I guarantee you it's a prank. We've had some of our people remain here all afternoon after we did the first sweep, so now we're looking for a package, a briefcase, something portable. There's a lot of kooks out there. Give us a few minutes to double-check everything."

Earl went on stage to alerte the audience that a routine and last-minute check of the facility was underway for their own security.

"We shouldn't be but just a few minutes more. President Trump has not arrived as of this time anyway, so we're not slowing things down. We'll let you know as soon as it's complete and the President arrives."

Ten minutes later, Butch got a call on his radio alerting him that everything was all clear. He turned again to Earl. "It's clean. Your meeting is good to go. I'll have my guys remain here for a while, just in case. We've got some pretty sophisticated detection equipment with us. If anybody tries to get in here late with an explosive, we'll know it. So, you've got the go-ahead to get on with your meeting."

General Morrison looked at his watch. "If Trump doesn't show up real soon, there's not going to be a meeting."

A familiar voice came up directly behind him. "How very little faith you have in me, General Morrison. I wouldn't miss this for the world. I'm ready for my presentation right now. Hang around, Claiborne. You're probably going to hear your name mentioned a few times. I'll head on to the stage now."

He turned to Earl. "I assume you're the manager here?"

"Yes, sir, Mr. President. I want to tell you how happy I am that you're still alive and with us today. Follow me and I'll introduce you."

"Lead on."

General Morrison spoke up with a loud and commanding voice. "I don't think you're going to want to give this speech, Mr. President."

"And why would that be?"

"Some of the people here with me would undoubtedly be hurt by what you intend to say."

"And what people would that be?"

Morrison turned to Lieutenant Drexler and motioned him to bring out some "guests." Four soldiers carrying M-16s, flanked by the same number of Secret Service agents, walked out to the center of the room escorting the surprise guests. The soldiers and agents surrounded Donald Jr. and Ivanka Trump. The younger Trumps had their mouths taped shut and their hands tied behind their backs. Directly behind them was Jim's son from West Point, also tightly bound.

"Why, Mr. President, you seem very surprised. You didn't really think we'd let your own kids die in that blaze in Georgia, did you? They are far too valuable for that to happen. They're here to make sure you come quietly with us. The crowd out front will be told that they were held by the same group of conspirators that took down Air Force One. A very sad time in the country and a very big news story. You see, Donald, the world is a lot bigger than one man, or even one country. I'm tasked with keeping the world safe and you're a threat to that order. You've caused me a lot of trouble over the past week. I'm not in a mood to let this go on. So, my guards will escort you and your kids, and our young cadet here back to the Pentagon. We have a trip planned for all of you together. We'll talk more about that later in a more secure place. OK, Drexler, let's get this group out of here."

Lieutenant Drexler motioned to the guards to move the Trumps and James toward the waiting cars. They didn't respond in any way. He looked closely at them and then at the Capitol Police who were closing in around him. He lowered his arm and made a move to grab his .45 automatic from his holster. No sooner had his hand touched the pistol grip than Jim Grimshaw took his own weapon and pistol-whipped him violently on the side of his head and face. Drexler fell to the floor. The Capitol Police immediately bound his hands with plastic handcuffs behind his back. General Morrison took a step backward in disbelief at the action against one of his key officers. He looked over at the men guarding the Trumps. He was starting to realize that he didn't recognize any of their faces.

He gave another command, much stronger. "Arrest that man, bring him with us. Grab Drexler and let's get these people out here."

He turned to two Capitol Police officers standing on either side of Donald.

"Grab him and take him to the van outside."

The disbelieving general moved his hand toward his own service revolver. He had been in combat many times and would not be easily frightened by a few Capitol Police who hadn't fired a pistol in the past ten years unless at a range. Again, Grimshaw moved forward and grabbed his arm before he could remove his pistol from its holster. He relished the opportunity to confront the traitor.

"Do you really want to play chicken with the devil, General? My three tours of 'Nam weren't in a command tent twenty miles from the lines. I was a Ranger for all of my twenty-three years and my time was always on the wrong side of the line. A turncoat like you wouldn't be wise to give me the chance to crack his skull. Because frankly, I'd just love to do it."

Now shaken, the general spoke to the Capitol Police again. "You, men. Arrest these people now. Don't make me tell you again. That's a direct order from the head of the Army. Do you hear what I'm telling you?"

Again, the officers didn't respond.

Donald then spoke. "There's been a development, Morrison. I think the military would call it a 'change of command.' You see, your staff has been sidetracked. They're confined to a small room in the basement as we speak. A group of real American patriots accompanied me here today. Why even the Capitol Police Bomb Disposal Unit your men let onto the grounds is actually all retired military veterans, many are Special Forces. They're not real happy with what you've done to their country. They're going to escort you and your men outside and into a waiting bus. You're going to be held at a federal prison until your court-martial. I was never a supporter of capital punishment so, if I have my way, you'll have a lifetime behind bars to plan your next adventure."

Morrison's facial expression showed equal parts of rage, indignation and fear. He wasn't leaving without Donald Trump hearing his thoughts. "You might think this is over with, Trump. But it's not even close to being done. The people you're crossing today are still very much in control of everything. You're just in charge of one old VFW hall and a couple dozen old men. You'll be lucky if you make it to a safe place to sleep tonight. Don't close your eyes. They'll be coming for you, and that's a fact."

Donald walked over to the disgraced and fuming general. He placed his face about six inches directly in front of Morrison's. "You're wrong, Morrison. I don't think I run this country and I know you don't. The people run the United States of America. They chose me to look out for their interests and that's exactly what I'm going to do. And there's not just a couple dozen of them. There're around four hundred million of them. They're hard-working and honest, every size, shape, age and color. They don't like being lied to. And they especially don't like it when people like you think they can steal what belongs to them. I'm about to go explain to them exactly what's been going on in Washington. There won't be enough rat holes to go around when the treasonous scoundrels start trying to jump ship tonight. That's OK though, because we've plenty of places to put 'em. You might be sharing a cell with some of them very soon. Butch, until you hear something different directly from me, you are in charge of the Capitol Police right now. All of it. Now have some of your people get him out of my sight."

"Yes, sir, Mr. President. My pleasure."

"And, Jim, please have your men take the bonds off my kids and your son."

As they were freed, Donald went over to his kids and embraced them tightly. "Where are Eric, Tiffany and Barron?"

"Safe. They were hidden in Florida by friends. There's a group of vets, just like these men, watching their every move. They're in the best hands possible. For a while, we thought it was all over. They tried to make us think you were dead."

Donald Jr. looked at his father. "And Mom?"

"She's safe. Friends in the Middle East have been looking out for her from the moment Air Force One was destroyed. We'll have her safely back home tomorrow. Now, let's go tell the public what's been going on here. Jim, you and your son come with me. There's a group of people out front waiting to hear all about how I got here and what's going on."

Kevin Marshall entered the room and walked over to Butch Watson and Grimshaw. He announced in what must have been a flashback for all of them, "Sir, I'm retired Gunny Sergeant Kevin Marshall. Currently assigned to Florence, South Carolina. I'm here with approximately six hundred other men from all up and down the coast. With a little more notice, we could have had even more. We're here to offer our full support and protection for the President. We know we should have kept quiet about all this, but we were just afraid that you might have a problem and not enough manpower to back you up and make this happen. So, we're here for you. All surrounding areas outside of the hall are secure. We are in control for the moment unless Morrison or any of his henchman got out a call for support."

"That didn't happen. They were taken by surprise."

Donald Trump walked to the podium to thunderous applause and noise. The popular President they had been told was dead was once again in front of them. After an extended celebration, the crowd settled down to hear their President speak.

"My friends, I cannot express with words how grateful I am to be standing up here in front of you tonight. Were it not for some incredible heroics by a number of men and women in this country and great friends overseas, it wouldn't have happened. America has a cancer growing inside of it from people who don't see our country the way you and I do. They see the world as one big corporation, and they want to control it. They will stop at nothing. They start and end wars. They ruin lawful governments, destroy their leaders, and even assassinate them if they don't move out of their way. Air Force One was not destroyed by terrorists in the Middle East. It was ordered destroyed by men sitting in big offices in high-rise buildings right here in our nation's capital. They have their tentacles embedded deeply into every branch of our government, our military and throughout other countries all over the world. They feel invincible. And this isn't a new development. This has been a slow, deliberate and well-executed plot that they've been working day and night to accomplish for over fifty years. Well, I was fortunate. I had friends who rescued me and the First Lady, who I'm thrilled to tell you is alive and well. She will be joining us here tomorrow."

Another rousing applause went on for several minutes with the mention of the of popular First Lady's return to the United States.

"So, what do we do? How do we get rid of these traitors? You've taken one big step already. You elected a president who still believes in the greatness of this country. I believe in its people, its institutions, and its history. Repeatedly, we've been tested as a nation. When it looked like we might fail, you rose up against the corruption that was edging into your government at every level. You instinctively know when things are headed in the wrong direction, and you stop what you are doing to grab these people by the throat and shake them to their roots. Tomorrow, I will be back in the Oval Office. I will be taking the steps I think you would want me to. I will find every last one of these conspirators and see that they pay the ultimate price for the betrayal they perpetrated upon our country. I wouldn't be here tonight if it weren't for a group of men who risked everything to answer the call of their country. Most of them have been doing it all their adult lives. They are the veterans of our armed forces. They are older now, anywhere from about sixty to over eighty years old. When they found out what was happening, they offered to lay their lives on the line once again to save their country. But they are not young enough to stay on perpetual guard against the type of enemy we're dealing with today. They need for us and our younger generations to get serious about freedom, learn our country's true history, and relieve them of their duty stations. It is our turn to take the watch. We've counted on them being there for too long. It's now time we watch over them. From here on out, I'll be doing just that. You elected me to protect what you hold dear and with God as my witness, that's exactly what I'm going to do. I will stay vigilant, stand up for what is right in America, and take down those who would destroy us. Together, we will never let them take charge of anything we value. As I appoint all new department heads and key staff members at every branch of government starting right now, look at your local officials and ask yourselves, are these the people that we want looking out for us? If not, then I ask you to take the same steps wherever you are to rid yourselves of this cancer. Let's all work as one to make America great again. And to those of you listening to me tonight, if you were involved in any of this, you need to make good on your goodbyes because we'll be knocking on your doors very quickly. We love you, America! Goodnight!"

After Donald finished his speech, there was deafening applause inside and outside of the hall thanks to audio speakers set up on the hall's lawn. A large convoy escorted Donald Trump to the White House from the hall. The group of veterans protecting him had swelled to over a thousand men and women. A number of the current military had quickly joined their ranks once they realized it truly was President Trump. There was no resistance at the gates to the White House. In less than thirty minutes, there were satellite trucks for blocks surrounding the White House.

The Trumps rested safely inside the historic residence that night for the first time since Donald had taken office. Members of his personal security force now controlled the quarters and spent the entire night removing monitors, cameras, microphones and any other monitoring devices they could find.

By sunrise, the other generals on the Joint Chiefs had been arrested in their homes and offices. More than one involved officer and agency head saw fit to end their lives on their own rather than wait for the total disgrace that was imminent.

Melania Trump was flown home within hours in a military Galaxy C5A, accompanied by a complete squadron of F16s. She received a hero's welcome at the airport and fell into the immediate embraces of her kids and Donald. It was not just a monumental day for the country. It was an exceptional moment in time for their entire family.

***

Capitol Police and National Guardsmen surrounded the gleaming tower just outside Washington D.C. A heavily armed squad of officers in SWAT gear, carrying automatic weapons, made their way to the luxurious suite on the top floor. Repeated pounding on the door and commands to open the office went unanswered. Realizing they would have to handle it on their own, the police forced the door open. They all took a knee as they entered, pointing their rifles at every corner not knowing what to expect inside. They were somewhat dismayed when they looked throughout the oversized suite that occupied the entire top floor of the building. Other than furniture, it was completely bare. There was no doubt to those who had conducted his interrogation that Morrison had sent them to the correct location. He was a difficult subject and it took just over six hours to loosen him up. It was interesting to note that waterboarding, which he had so vehemently opposed in public was the first step used in encouraging his cooperation. Unfortunately, it was not nearly as severe as what had to be done to get him onboard with finding the rats and all their holes.

✳ ✳ ✳

Later in the week, Donald Trump gave one of the most powerful speeches ever presented by a sitting President. He spoke from a podium erected on the Washington Mall. The crowd was the largest ever to gather at the historic venue. In the late afternoon breeze, the flags of dozens of military regiments could readily be seen throughout the crowd. They represented the many groups of retired vets who were not only in attendance, but also without whom the event would not have occurred. For weeks, the purging of the government would continue.

General Morrison's trial uncovered the vast extent of corruption that had infiltrated the ranks of virtually every agency and bureau in the government and at every level. Evidence revealed during the trial resulted in the arrest and incarceration of hundreds of high-profile politicians and bureaucrats at the federal, state and even local levels. Heads rolled at the major media outlets as a disgusted public demanded change at all ends of the spectrum. Federal prisons would be at full occupancy for many years to come. General Morrison would spend the rest of his life behind bars and his name would become synonymous with betrayal to an extent rivaling that of Benedict Arnold.

Undoubtedly, some involved in the conspiracy slipped through the cracks. There were also those who would remain under suspicion by the President for the remainder of their lives. Donald would spend the rest of his presidency trying to reestablish the credibility of the government to the American people. It would be a full generation before they could completely feel that the government was once again, "of the people, by the people and for the people."

***

Singapore is a modern, wealthy megalopolis. Some have said it's much like New York City, except clean and well run. It certainly is prosperous with most of the world's great corporations having a presence in one of the hundreds of skyscrapers throughout the city. It's a showplace for extreme capitalism. Inside one of the tallest skyscrapers in the heart of the business district, a meeting was taking place late in the evening. Through the floor to ceiling windows, the brilliant lights of the city appeared to be a galaxy all their own. Those present considered themselves to be the sun, around which these bright planets revolved. A tall, gray-haired man sat on the front of an ornate mahogany desk. He looked intently at each of those present in the room as he spoke.

"Yes, I cannot deny we suffered a setback. Donald Trump proved to be a lot more resilient than we gave him credit for. He has re-stacked the deck throughout the central government and military in the States. That ended a very long and successful run for us. He has also made it very difficult for us to run our concern there. It will undoubtedly be that way for some time. But people have short memories. The universities are still full of those overeducated and not-too-smart 'intelligencia' who assist us by brainwashing their charges with socialism and other Marxist propaganda. They actually despise what built America. They just don't get it and even Trump won't be able to get control of them. One generation, maybe two generations from now, Americans will once again grow complacent, lose their appetite for hard work, forget their history, and become lax in watching over their institutions. Then when the time is right, we'll re-establish ourselves there again. This is not a short-term venture, as you all know. We are in this for the long haul, the very long haul. Singapore is a wonderful place that embraces wealth and power. I would call it an incubator for a concern such as ours. We'll do very well here. Tomorrow I meet with several military dictators from countries that not only want our support, but need our help in marketing their natural resources. These countries all contain vast quantities of the world's lifeblood, oil. We know that industry better than anyone does. There is a great opportunity for us to vastly grow our operations. In a few years, we'll be bigger and more powerful than ever. And, in a few more years, we'll test the waters again in the United States. I think that about covers our agenda for this meeting. Good day, gentlemen.

Epilogue

Donald Trump served two terms as President. He was considered by most Americans to be the savior of their country. He reinstated the rule of law, enforced the nation's borders and through his Attorney General upheld the rule of law in an equal and fair manner guided by the Constitution. With his business savvy and influence, America re-emerged as the world's leading economy bringing stability and an improving lifestyle to all Americans, not just those favored by the ruling party.

There is a statement that was quoted often by John F. Kennedy, "A rising tide floats all boats." Using that reason, even those who wanted to change the entire direction of the country benefited from the growing economy. Universities received more money and as a result, even the radical professors who lived off tax dollars while defaming those who actually generated money and paid them, grew stronger in their ivory towers. Donald Trump succeeded in getting the United States of America back on the course envisioned by its Founding Fathers.

While in office, President Trump saw to it that the government dramatically increased funding for the Veteran's Administration with a special emphasis on contributing to the Veterans of Foreign Wars, or VFW halls across the nation. He often spoke in their small meeting halls and never failed to pay tribute to those who came to his aide and helped the country get rid of the parasites that were living in its capital while disguised as our leaders.

Jim Grimshaw became the National President of the Rangers Association and spoke tirelessly of the need to stay on watch and hold elected leaders accountable, even on small matters. During Donald Trump's Presidency, Grimshaw's son rose through the ranks of the Army to that of Major. He and his father both received the Presidential Freedom Award for their undying loyalty to the country and the heroic effort they put forth in saving it.

"The Price of Freedom is Eternal Vigilance" – Used by many of our Founding Fathers but most often identified as a quote from Thomas Jefferson.

About the Author

Les Pendleton lives in historic New Bern, North Carolina. His writing style conveys the influence of his career in motion pictures. Many people share their impression that reading his novels feels as if you are watching the characters come to life on the silver screen. Actual locations in coastal North Carolina are featured in many of his books. His writing spans a wide array of genres from action adventure, romance, historical fiction, suspense-filled mysteries to autobiographies. Les spends every free moment with his family and friends sailing in Pamlico Sound and along the Atlantic Coast.

Learn more about the author at www.lespendleton.com

* * *

Thank you for reading this novel.
We invite you to share your thoughts and reactions
by going to **Amazon.com/author/lespendleton**
and posting a review.

Essie Press

Made in the USA
Columbia, SC
12 November 2022

70714171R00169